"GAELIC MADE EASY"

A Guide to Gaelic for Beginners

PART 2

COMPRISING 10 LESSONS IN GAELIC

Written and Compiled by

John M. Paterson

GAIRM PUBLICATIONS
29 Waterloo Street,
Glasgow G2 6BZ, Scotland

FOREWARD

This is the second part of a series of lessons published by the Gaelic League of Scotland for the benefit of their students and others who are studying the Gaelic. The lessons appeared originally in AN CEUM, a monthly now discontinued. The method of instruction employed was initiated by the League and has been found to be successful over a period of years.

In this, the fifth edition of Part II, typographical errors have been corrected and, where desirable, explanations have been made fuller. The text is substantially the same.

First Edition..........................1952
Third Edition (Revised).............1954
Fourth Edition (Revised)...........1990
This impression.....................1998

GAELIC MADE EASY PART 2

ISBN: 0-57970-549-9 text only
0-88432-443-5 text and cassettes
1-57970-124-8 text and cds

This edition published by Audio Forum
One Orchard Park Road, Madison, CT 06443 U.S.A.
www.audioforum.com

Printed in the United States of America

SOUND TABLE

A as in CAT. Never as in MATE.
E as in THEY or MET. Never as in ME.
I as in MACHINE or FIT. Never as in FIRE.
O as in GO or GOT.
U as in PUT or BUT. Never as in FUEL.
AO like EH-OO said quickly or as EU in NEUVE in French.
PH as F. Compare PHOTO in English.
BH and MH as V in VAT.
CH as in LOCH.
DH and GH as GH in UGH! back in the throat.
SH and TH as H in HAT.
FH is silent except in three words FHEIN (hayn) self; FHUAIR (hoo-ir) found or got and FHATHAST (ha-hast) yet, where it has the sound of H.
IS as IS in MISSION i.e. ISH; but IS meaning 'is' in English is sounded ISS as in HISS.
SI as SI in MISSION i.e. SHI.
IDH and IGH as EE.
DHI and GHI as YE.
ANN sounds both 'Ns' though it is often sounded as if A-OON.
L before A, O, U is broad like LL in CALLING or the sound of THL.
MH and BH often sounded like W in middle of a word, though, like V would also be correct.
I and E, when the second letters of a word, often sound like Y: e.g. DIURA (dyoora) Jura where DI is almost a 'j' sound. CEANN (Kya-oon) head, but when an action-word is in past time this 'y' sound does not appear. LION! (lyeeon) FILL! but LION (leeon) FILLED.

Note.—We use the 'j' sound in the imitated pronunciation.

C in or at the end of a word is often sounded as CHK thus MAC as if it were MACHK, the CH sounded as in LOCH.
RT is often sounded as RST.
D and T. Get tongue well against back of upper front teeth. T is almost TH.
B and P and F. More forcibly than in English.
G well back in throat. GOT would be like UG-OT said in one syllable.

IMITATED PRONUNCIATION

Sound CH as in loCH, ch as in church. O as in sO, o as in got, ich as in which ; j as in jilt ; ing as in sing ; ay as in day but a dull sound at the end of a word ; oo as in moon ; eh as in eh!

Only an approximate pronunciation has been aimed at. Anything more complex or detailed would only confuse the learner.

LESSON 11

The Gaelic words for My, Thy and so on are much like the English. Here they are. MO (**mO**), My. DO (**dO**), Thy. AR, Our. UR (**oor**), Your. Sometimes UR is written BHUR (**voor**). A stands for His or Her, and AN (written AM before B, F, M, P), Their.

Notice that MO, DO, and A meaning His, sharpen if possible the first letter of the following word: the others do not.

Examples—MO BHORD, My table. DO CHAT, Thy Cat. A MHATHAIR (**a va-hir**) His mother. But A MATHAIR (**a ma-hir**), Her mother. AR CAR, Our car. UR PEITEAG (**pay-chag**), Your waistcoat. AN TAIGH, Their house. But again, AM BAILE, Their town.

These last two might also mean The house, The town, and so we often hear AN TAIGH ACA, The house at them or Their house, and AM BAILE ACA, Their town. This usage has become common and so we find AN TAIGH AGAM, My house: AN CAR AIGE, His car, and so on.

Example—THA AN CAR AIGE SEAN. His car is old. SEAN (**shen**) old.

Before words beginning with a vowel, A, meaning Her, takes an H-, and AR and UR (BHUR) an N-.

Examples — A H-UBHAL (**a-hooal**), Her apple. UBHAL (**oo-al**), Apple. UBHLAN (**oo-lan**), Apples. A H-UINNEAG (**a hoonyag**), Her window.

AR N-ARAN, Our bread. UR N-AIRGIOD (**oor nerra-gud**), Your money. You sometimes find MO and DO written M' and D' before vowels. CHUIR MI

M'AD AIR MO CHEANN, I put my hat on my head (**CHyaoon**). AD (**at**) hat.

Instead of MATH good, we often use DEAGH (**jayoo**); also instead of DONA bad, we may use DROCH (**droCH**). These two new words can only be used in front of the name-word, never after: and further, they sharpen it if possible. Thus DEAGH BHORD (**jayoo vord**) a good table: DROCH BHORD, a bad table. We cannot say THA AM BORD DEAGH (or DROCH) but we can say THA AM BORD MATH (or DONA).

One little point in pronunciation is well worth noting here. Take for example NIGHEAN (**nyeean**) girl or daughter and LEABHAR (**lyOr**) book. After MO, DO, A meaning his, we drop this "y" sound in pronunciation. Thus MO NIGHEAN (**mO neean**) my daughter, A LEABHAR (**a lOar**) his book; but A NIGHEAN (**a nyee-an**) her daughter, A LEABHAR (**a-lyOr**) her book. AR, UR, AN (AM) like A, her, keep the "y" sound. UR NIGHEAN (**oor nyee-an**) your daughter.

Faclair

FACLAIR (**faCH-klir**) vocabulary.
CARAID (**kar-ij**) friend.
BEATHA (**beh-ha**) life; also used to mean welcome.
FREAGAIRT (**frek-irt** or—**irsht**) answer.
STOL (**stol**) stool.
FAINNE (**fan-ya**) ring.
GOIRT (**gorsht**) sore. Note also, BAINNE GOIRT sour milk.
RATHAIDEAN (**ra-hij-an**) roads.
BARAIL (**bar-il**) opinion. BUIL (**bool**) use.
LUIDHEAR (**loo-yer**) chimney.
'NA THEINE (**na hayn-ya**) on fire (lit in its fire).
FEARG (**fer-ag**) anger.
CHUALA (**CHooa-la**) heard.
MAR THACHAIR (**mar haCH-ir**) How (or what) happened.
TOIT (**totch**) smoke.
RUD (U as in put) thing.

MILL (**meel**) spoil, ruin.
SRAC! (**sraCHk**) tear!
SRACTE (**sraCHk-chay**) torn.
SPORAN purse. SPARAN is a rare form.

Gaelic to English

Mo bhrogan. A charaid. An caraid agam. A caraid. Do bheatha. Ur beatha. Ur n-iasg. Bhur taigh. An taigh agaibh. An each. A dhorus. Mo fhreagairt. M' (Mo) fhion. Am fion agam. Na taigh-ean aca. An duine aice. Mo leabhar. Do sporan. A nighean. An nighean aice. A stol. An stol aige. An stol aice. A fainne. Am fiodh. Am fiodh aca.

Tha mo cheann goirt. Bha a pheiteag sracte. Shrac e a pheiteag. Mhill e a bhrogan air na droch rathaidean. Tha droch bharail agam air. Chuir Mairi a h-airgiod gu deagh bhuil. Chuir mo mhac beag an luidhear 'na theine. Thainig an nighean agam a steach bho a h-obair agus chuir i as e. Bha fearg air an duine agam an uair a chuala e mar thachair. Dh'fhag an toit a h-uile rud anns an taigh salach.

Translation

My shoes. His friend. My friend. Her friend. Thy life (familiar form): or Welcome! Your life (used to strangers and elders): or Welcome! Your fish. Your house. Your house. Their horse. His door. My answer. My wine. My wine. Their houses. Her husband (man). My book. Thy purse. His (or her) daughter. Her daughter. His (or her) stool. His stool. Her stool. Her ring. Their (or The) wood. Their wood.

My head is sore. His waistcoat was torn. He tore his waistcoat. He ruined his shoes on the bad roads. I have a bad opinion of (on) him. Mary put her money to good use. My little son put (set) the chimney on fire. My daughter came in from her work and she put it out. My husband was angry (anger was on my husband) when he heard what happened. The smoke made (left) everything in the house dirty.

LESSON 12

There is a very curious way in Gaelic of using the words Standing, sitting, sleeping and lying down. Take the word CADAL which means sleeping. Now we cannot say THA E A' CADAL for He is sleeping but we must say THA E AN A ('NA) CHADAL, word for word, He is in his sleep. Notice that in English we may also say He is asleep. Take again the word SEASAMH (**shayss-av**), standing. BHA SINN AN AR ('NAR) SEASAMH, We were in our standing, i.e. We were standing. Of course we might have said SHEAS SINN (**hayss sheeng**), We stood, as in English. You will notice That AN is written 'N when followed by MO, DO, A, etc., and that AN MO is shortened to 'NAM and AN DO to 'NAD. Here is a little table which may prove helpful. Always use the shortened forms which you see inside the brackets.

THA MI AN MO ('NAM) CHADAL, I am sleeping.
THA THU AN DO ('NAD) CHADAL, Thou art sleeping.
THA E AN A ('NA) CHADAL, He is sleeping.
THA I AN A ('NA) CADAL, She is sleeping.
THA SINN AN AR ('NAR) CADAL, We are sleeping.
THA SIBH AN UR ('NUR) CADAL, You are sleeping.
THA IAD AN AN ('NAN) CADAL, They are sleeping.

Remember that MO, DO, and A when it means His, sharpen the first letter of the following word if at all possible. LAIGHE (**la-ee**) lying, does not change: e.g. BHA E 'NA LAIGHE AIR AN LAR, He was lying on the ground. LAR, ground. The English phrase He came running is turned into Gaelic THAINIG E 'NA RUITH, He came in his running. RUITH (**roo-eeCH**) run! or running.

Faclair

SUIDH! (**soo-ee**) sit!
SUIDHE (**soo-ya**), sitting.
TEINE, fire.
TAOBH (**toov**), side.
RI TAOBH AN TEINE, at (the) side of the fire. Note that in this phrase and in all similar, the first of the two "the's" is never translated in Gaelic.
FAD AN LATHA (or LA), throughout the day, i.e. all day.
LATHA (**la-a**) day. SEAS! (**shayss**) stand!
SEASAMH (**shayss-av**), standing.
LAIGH! (**laee**) lie down!
LAIGHE (**la-ya**), lying down. Both LAIGH and LAIGHE are often spelt with a "U" instead of an "A".
CAIDIL! (**kaj-eel**) sleep!
CADAL (**kadl**), sleeping or sleep.
SIN! (**sheen**) stretch!
SINEADH (**sheen-yuGH**), stretching.
CUL (**kool**), back. AIG CUL AN TAIGHE, at the back of the house.
TAIGH (**ta-ee**), house.
TAIGHE (**ta-ya**), of a house.
MUR (**moor**), if not, unless. It is followed by the second form of the action-word, 'EIL, ROBH, BI, etc.
CREAG (**krayk**), rock. CREAGAN, rocks.
SGIAN AGUS SGOR (**skor**), knife and fork.
UISDEAN (**ooshjan**) Hugh.
GLEIDH! (**glay**) keep!
EIRICH! (**ay-reeCH**) rise!
EIRIGH (**ay-ree**) rising.
TRAIGH (**tra-ee**), shore.
TOG ORT! (**tOk-orst**) lift on you! i.e. get a move on!
SIN AGAD (AGAIBH used to seniors) IAD, there you have them. Lit. There at you them.
SUIL (**sool**) eye.
SUILEAN (**soolan**) eyes.
COINNICH! (**kOn-yeeCH**) meet!
TROM (**trowm**), heavy.
GLAN, clean.
GU GLAN, cleanly.

Gaelic to English

Tha Iain 'na sheasamh aig an dorus. Bha mo mhathair 'na suidhe ri taobh an teine. Chunnaic am maighstir gun robh Mairi 'na cadal. Bha e fuar 'nar n-eaglais an diugh. C'ait' am bheil na clachan ud a nis? Tha iad 'nan laighe aig cul an taighe. Mur bi sinn ag iasgach, bidh sinn 'nar sineadh air na creagan aig an traigh. Eirich, Iain, tog ort agus na bi 'nad laighe an sin fad an la. Chuir sinn ar n-im agus ar n-uibhean do'n bhaile ach ghleidh Mairi a h-im agus a h-uibhean aig an taigh. Nach 'eil sgian agus sgor aig Uisdean? Sin agad iad air a' bhord, fo do shuilean. Choinnich Morag a h-athair agus a mathair anns a' bhaile an de. Chaidil mi gu trom an raoir. Shuidh i anns a' chathair. Ruith an gille suas an t-sraid. Chaidil i fad an latha. Bha i 'na cadal fad an latha.

Translation

John is standing at the door. My mother was sitting beside the fire. The master saw that Mary was sleeping. It was cold in our church to-day. Where are yon stones now? They are lying at the back of the house. If we are not fishing, we will be stretched out on the rocks at the shore. Rise John, bestir yourself, and don't be lying there all day. We sent our butter and our eggs to the town but Mary kept her butter and her eggs at home. Has Hugh not a knife and fork? There they are on the table under your eyes. Morag met her father and her mother in the town yesterday. I slept heavily last night. She sat in the chair. The boy ran up the street. She slept all day. She was asleep (or sleeping) all day.

LESSON 13

From past lessons we know that a phrase like I am striking is turned into Gaelic by THA MI A' BUALADH (**booal-uGH**) which really means I am at striking, the A' being short for AIG (At). Mary is striking John would be THA MAIRI A' (AIG) BUALADH IAIN. If we know who is being struck we could quite well say Mary is striking him. This is turned in a slightly different, and neater, way in Gaelic by saying THA MAIRI AIG A BHUALADH (**vooal-uGH**), i.e. Mary is at his striking. Something of this kind is seen in English when we say The workmen were at its removal (a fallen wall). A few examples will make the point clearer. You might perhaps notice how AIG and the word following it are shortened into one single word.

THA MAIRI 'GAM (AIG MO) BHUALADH, Mary is striking me.

THA M. 'GAD (AIG DO) BHUALADH, M. is striking thee (or you).

THA M. 'GA (AIG A) BHUALADH, M. is striking him.

THA M. 'GA (AIG A) BUALADH, M. striking her.

THA M. 'GAR (AIG AR) BUALADH, M. is striking us.

THA M. 'GUR (AIG UR) BUALADH, M. is striking you.

THA M. 'GAM (AIG AM) BUALADH, M. is striking them.

Remember that MO, DO and A meaning His sharpen the first letter of the next word and that AN becomes AM before B, F, M, P.

Instead of Mary we might say She, and this would run.

THA I 'GAM BHUALADH, She is striking me. And so on.

If Mary was striking herself, we would add FHEIN (**hayn**) Self. THA MAIRI (or I) 'GA BUALADH FHEIN.

Often you have two ways of turning such phrases as above. For instance, CHA ROBH MI 'GA THUIGSINN (or CHA DO THUIG MI E) AN UAIR A BHA E A' BRUIDHINN I wasn't understanding (or did not understand) him when he was speaking. BRUIDHINN (**broo-ying**), Speak! or Speaking.

And now, to change the subject. A boy in Gaelic is BALACH or GILLE and A girl CAILEAG. The Boy is AM BALACH or AN GILLE but The Girl AN CHAILEAG or more shortly A' CHAILEAG. Gaelic divides its name-words into two groups, one like BALACH or GILLE and the other like CAILEAG which has its first letter sharpened wherever possible after the word for The. This curious way of dividing up name-words is found in other languages besides Gaelic, only instead of sharpening the first letter of the word they alter the word for 'The'. And it doesn't matter whether you are speaking about persons or things or even qualities such as Speed, colour, truth, etc. For instance Le Train is The Train in French but La Table The Table. Le has become La. In German we say Der Hunger The Hunger, but Die Farbe The Colour.

Why these things should be we don't quite know, but most languages have them. Those who write grammars call them Masculine and Feminine words. This is not a very good way of distinguishing them, for Tables, Trains, Hunger and so on have nothing to do with sex. We shall therefore call them simply Class 1 and Class 2 words. So we shall write BALACH (1) and CAILEAG (2), but if you have studied a foreign language, keep in mind that Class (1) will represent the words you called Masculine and Class (2) those you called Feminine.

Note that a word which describes a Class 2 name-word is, if possible, sharpened. Thus CAILEAG MHOR, A big girl. A' CHAILEAG MHOR, The big girl. CAS, A foot, A' CHAS, The foot. A' CHAS BHEAG, The little foot. BEINN (**baynn**), A Ben or Peak. A' BHEINN ARD, The high peak. You can't, of course, sharpen a vowel, in this case the A of ARD.

SRON (**sron**) nose. SRON FHADA (**sron ada**) a long nose. But AN T-SRON FHADA (**an tron ada**) the long nose. Observe how these Class 2 words beginning with S take a T after AN, the. This T makes the S silent. Thus again SRAID (**sraj**) 2. street. AN T-SRAID (**an traj**) the street. If, however, the S is followed by G, M, P. T (**GuMPoT**) there is no change, e.g. AN SGOIL 2. the school. AN SPOG 2. (**spog**) the claw. Nor do Class I. words change either, e.g. AN SAOR the joiner. AN SRUTH (**sroo**) the stream.

Note, however, that these S words (except the **GuMPoT** variety), whether they belong to Class 1 or Class 2, put in a "T" when they are used with AIG at, AIR on, DO to, LEIS with and so on.

Example—AIR AN T-SRAID (**traj**) Class 2. On the street. AIG AN T-SRUTH (**troo**) Class 1. At the stream.

Faclair

CEOL (**kyol**) 1. music.
BINN (**beeng**) tuneful, sweet.
CLANN (**klaoon**) 2. children.
CAOL (**kool**) narrow.
CEAPAIRE (**kep-a-ra**) 1. sandwich.
CIURR (**kyoor**) hurt!
CIURRADH (**kyoor-uGH**) hurting.
CAISE (**kash-a**) 1. cheese.
UR (**oor**) new, fresh: also "your".
GORM (**gor-um**), blue.
GIULAIN! (**gyoo-layn**) carry!
GIULAN (**gyoo-lan**) carrying.
GAOTH (**goo**) 2. wind.
LAIDIR (**la-jir**) strong.
DROCHAID (**droCH-ij**) 2. bridge.
DRUIM (**drooeem**) 1. back.
AN DA CHUID (**Chooj**), both.
IOMAIN (**eem-ayn**) drive!
IOMAIN, driving.
MUIR (**mooir**) 2. sea.
TOIRT (**to-irst**) taking.
PEIGI (**payg-ee**) Peggy.
GLE (**glay**) very, sharpens the first letter of the next word.
ANN (**a-oon**), in being: with MADUINN, FEASGAR and LA it is not translated into English.

Gaelic to English

Loch fada. An loch fada. Clann bheag. A' chlann bheag. Ceol binn. An ceol binn. Bonnach milis. Am bonnach milis. Brog ur. A' bhrog ur. Sruth mor. An sruth mor. Suil ghorm. An t-suil ghorm. Drochaid chaol. An drochaid chaol. Feasgar math ann. Maduinn mhath ann. Oidhche mhath leibh. These last three are salutations.

Co bha 'gad bhualadh, Iain? Bha Peigi mhor. Tha ur cota deas. Am bi sibh 'ga thoirt air falbh am maireach? Tha mi a' faicinn gle mhath nach 'eil e 'gam chreidsinn. Bidh sinn 'gur faicinn (said at parting with a friend). Bha Anna bheag sgith agus bha a h-athair 'ga guilan air a dhruim. An gabh thu ceapaire caise Iain, no bonnach milis? Gabhaidh mi an da chuid. Tha acras mor orm. Bha eagal oirnn gum bitheadh (or biodh) a' ghaoth laidir 'gar n-iomain a mach air a' mhuir. Tha a chas goirt agus tha a bhrog 'ga ciurradh. An t-sraid fhada. Tha an t-sraid fada. Bha a' chaileag gle bheag.

Translation

A long loch. The long loch. Little children. The little children. Sweet music. The sweet music. A sweet-cake. The sweet-cake. A new shoe. The new shoe. A big stream. The big stream. A blue eye. The blue eye. A narrow bridge. The narrow bridge. Good evening! Good morning! Good night! Note LEIBH (**layv**), meaning "with you" does not appear in English.

Who was hitting you John? Big Peggy was. Your coat is ready. Will you be taking it away to-morrow? I see very well that he is not believing me. We'll be seeing you! Little Ann was tired and her father was carrying her on his back. Will you take a cheese-sandwich Iain, or a sweet-cake? I'll take both. I am very hungry (i.e. great hunger). We were afraid that the strong wind would be driving us out on the sea. His foot is sore and his shoe is hurting it. The long street. The street is long. The girl was very small.

LESSON 14

We have said that all name-words in Gaelic were divided up into two classes which the writers of grammars chose to call masculine and feminine, though we thought it better to call them Class 1 and Class 2. To avoid repeating the name-word too often in conversation we use E and I, E meaning He or It, and I meaning She or It. Thus we say.

THA AN TEINE BLATH, The fire is warm: or again THA E BLATH, It is warm.

BHA AM BALLA (or E) ARD, The wall (or It) was high.

TOG A' CHLACH MHOR, Lift the big stone.

TOG I, Lift it (referring to the stone).

THA CAS AN DUINE BRISTE, The foot ("of" understood) the man is broken.

THA I BRISTE, It is broken. BRISTE (**breesht-ya**), Broken. TEINE and BALLA as you will perhaps have noticed belong to Class 1 while CLACH and CAS belong to Class 2. Now the trouble is, in Gaelic as well as other languages, to know which name-words belong to Class 1 and which to Class 2. Here are one or two notes which may save you much trouble. First: Males, whether they be human beings or creatures, belong to Class 1. Secondly: Females, both human beings and creatures, belong to Class 2.

Generally speaking, words whose last vowel is A, O or U belong to Class 1 and those whose last vowel is "I" belong to Class 2. Include also in Class 2 most words ending in -AG or -ACHD. You will find now that you have accounted for a big number of the name-words in Gaelic. Some people find another method very helpful: e.g. BORD MOR, A big table. CLACH BHEAG, A small stone ; that is, using a describing word along with the name-word as a memory aid. Others would prefer to say AM BORD, The table. A' CHLACH, The stone. Or again, you might combine both ways.

Here are a few examples.

Class 1.—FEAR (**fer**), A man. PIOBAIR (**peebir**), A piper. EACH (**eCH**), A horse. COILEACH (**kull-aCH**), A cock. TINNEAS (**cheen-yas**), Sickness, or Disease. PAILTEAS (**palch-as**) Plenty. POSADH (**poss-uGH**), Marriage. SUIDHEACHADH (**soo-yaCH-uGH,** Situation BRON (**bron**), Sorrow. BUTH (**boo**), Shop. BODACH (**bOdach**), An old fellow. CEUM (**kaym**), A step.

Class 2.—BEAN (**ben**), A woman. CAILLEACH (**kal-yaCH**), An old wife. CEARC (**kyerk**), A hen. CUILEAG (**kool-ag**), A fly. CAILEAG (**kal-ag**), Girl. DUILLEAG (**dool-yag**), A leaf. LEABAG (**lyay-bag**), A flounder. MEARACHD (**mer-aCHk**), A mistake. RIOGHACHD (**ree-aCHk**), Kingdom. AOIGHEACHD (**oo-yaCHk**), Hospitality. MEIRLE (**mayr-la**), Theft. MAISE (**masha**), Beauty. DROCHAID (**droCH-ij**), Bridge. SUIL (**sool**), Eye. CANAIN (**kan-in**), Language. BANAIS (**banish**), Wedding-feast. TOINISG (**ton-ishk**), Sense or Understanding. TUR (**toor**) meaning much the same as Toinisg belongs to Class 1.

There are, of course, a number of name-words which don't just act according to rule but they are easy to get up. A few common ones are TAIGH, TEINE, BAILE, COIRE (**kora**), A kettle, which belong to Class 1.

CAS, CLANN, CLACH, BROG, LONG (**lOng**), a ship belong to Class 2.

When referring to This one or That one in Gaelic, whether persons or things, use FEAR (**fer**) for Class 1 words and TE (**chay**) for Class 2 words.

THA AM FEAR SEO TROM, This one (**BORD,** etc., Class 1) is heavy.

THA AN TE SEO DUBH This one (CEARC, etc., Class 2) is black. For 'ones' use AN FHEADHAINN (**an yO-ing**).

BHA AN FHEADHAINN SIN DONA, Those ones (persons or things) were bad.

FEADHAINN (**fyO-ing**) by itself means Some persons or things.

THA FEADHAINN DHIUBH MATH, Some of them are good. DHIUBH (**yoo**) of them. BH is silent.

Faclair

BRATACH (**bra-taCH**) 2. flag.
BEURLA SHASUNNACH (**bayr-la hassun-aCH**) 2. English. (BEURLA 2. really means speech, dialect).
BODHAR (**bO-ar**) deaf.
BHARR (**varr** nearly **farr**) off.
BRAISTE (**brash-chay**) 2. brooch.
BANARACH (**ban-ar-aCH**) 2. dairymaid.
BO (**bO**) 2. cow. CAS, steep.
CRUAIDH (**krooay**) hard.
CROITEAR (**krot-char**) 1. crofter.
FACLAIR (**faCHk-lar**) 1. dictionary, vocabulary.
GAIRDEAN (**gar-jan**) 1. arm.
GAIRDEANACH (**gar-jan-aCH**) with arms.
GEAL (**gyal**) bright.
GLAS, grey but green when referring to hills.
GRINN (**greeng**) fine.
GU PAILT (**goo palch**), plentifully.
MAOL (**mooal**), hornless, bald, blunt.
OBAIR (**Ob-ir**) 2. work.
SOCAIREACH (**soCHk-ir-aCH**) easy.
SLAT, 2. rod.
SEOL! (**shol**) sail! also a sail (Cl. 1).
IOMADH (**eema**) many a.
RUADH (**roo-uGH**) reddish.
REIC! (**rayCHk**) sell!
TOMADACH (**tOm-ad-aCH**) bulky.
TUATHANACH (**tooa-han-aCH**) 1. farmer.
DONN (**down**) brown.
LION! (**lyeen**) fill! but LION (**leen**) MI, I filled.
SLAN, whole, healthy.
SOLUS (**solus**) 1. light.
BAN, white.
SASUNNACH, English or Englishman.
DA, two, sharpens if possible the first letter of next word. It takes the form for one person or thing after it. Thus DA PHAIRC two parks, not DA PHAIRCEAN.

Gaelic to English

An uinneag bheag. A' bhratach ghorm. Cathair shocaireach. Ceann ruadh. Bo mhaol. Duine maol. Cathair ghairdeanach. Faclair tomadach. Sraid chaol.

Creag chas. Solus geal. Beurla Shasunnach. Cu glas. Cailleach bhodhar. Obair chruaidh. An traigh mhor. Slat ghrinn. An t-slat ghrinn. Caileag leisg. A' chaileag leisg.

Bha each ban agus each donn aig an tuathanach. Reic e am fear ban. Tha an uinneag beag. Tha an uinneag bheag briste (note these two sentences carefully). Ged tha an long bhoidheach sin sean, seolaidh i iomadh la fhathast. Tha da chanain againn an Alba, a' Ghaidhlig agus a' Bheurla Shasunnach. Tog an coire bharr an teine agus lion e le uisge fuar. Gabhaidh mi te de na braistean a tha agaibh air a' bhord sin. Dh'fhalbh a' chlann do'n traigh ach dh'fhag iad an te bheag aig an taigh. An d'fhuair (do fhuair) thu na h-uibhean an diugh Eilidh? Fhuair (omit the rest). Tha an fheadhainn seo slan ach tha an fheadhainn sin briste. Thuirt a' bhanarach gun robh bo mhaol aig a' chroitear agus gun robh i a' toirt bainne gu pailt. Tha feadhainn ag radh gum bi e a' falbh am maireach ach tha feadhainn eile ag radh nach bi.

Translation

The little window. The blue flag. An easy-chair. A red head. A hornless cow. A bald man. An arm-chair. A bulky dictionary. A narrow street. A steep rock. A bright light. English language. A grey dog. A deaf old woman. Hard work. The big shore. A fine rod. The fine rod. A lazy girl. The lazy girl.

The farmer had a white horse and a brown horse. He sold the white one. The window is small. The small window is broken. Though that bonnie ship is old, she will sail many a day yet. We have two languages in Scotland, Gaelic and English. Lift the kettle off the fire and fill it with cold water. I'll take one of the brooches that you have on that table. The children went off to the shore (beach) but they left the little one at home. Did you get the eggs to-day, Helen? I did (i.e. I got). These ones are whole but those ones are broken. The dairymaid said that the crofter had a hornless cow and that it was giving milk plentifully. Some are saying that he will be going to-morrow but others are saying that he will not (be).

LESSON 15

In the Gaidhealtachd (i.e. the Highlands) one passes the time of day with both friend and stranger on the road. It may be MADUINN MHATH ANN! (**ma-ting va'oon**) Good morning! THA LA BRIAGH ANN, AN DIUGH! It is a fine day, to-day; FEASGAR MATH ANN! (**fesk-ar ma'oon**) Good evening! We might further, on looking at the sky, say BIDH LA GASDA ANN, AM MAIREACH. It will be a fine day to-morrow. Now this little word ANN (**a-oon**) in the above phrase means "in existence" or "in being" or even loosely "in it" if we remember that the "it" does not refer to any person or thing in particular any more than does the "it" in "it rains." A few examples will help to make this clear.

THA E FUAR AN DIUGH, It is cold to-day.

THA FUACHD ANN, AN DIUGH, A coldness is in it (or in existence) to-day. It is chilly to-day.

BHA SNEACHD TROM ANN, AN DE. There was heavy snow (in being) yesterday.

SNEACHD (**snyeCHk**) 1. snow. FLICHNE (**fliCHnya**) 1. sleet. This comes from FLIUCH and SNEACHD.

BIDH FRAS ANN, AN UINE GHOIRID, There will be a shower in a short time.

GOIRID (**gur-ij**) means short, brief. UINE (**oonya**) 2. time. FRAS 2. shower.

ANN may also have the idea of place, as for instance AM BHEIL THU ANN, AIFRIG? Are you there, Euphemia? THA MI A' TIGHINN A' NIS. I am coming now.

AIFRIG (**efrig**) Euphemia.

'NUAIR A RAINIG MI AN TALLA CHA ROBH DUINE ANN. When I arrived at (or reached) the hall there was no person there.

TALLA (**tal-la**) 1. hall.

In Lesson 8 we saw how AIG, at, joined with MI to become AGAM, and so on for TU, E, I and the others. Now we can join up ANN in the same way. Here is a table of these forms.

ANNAM (**an-nam**), in me. ANNAD (**an-nad**), in thee or you. ANN (**a-oon**), in him or it. INNTE (**eenchay**), in her or it. ANNAINN (**an-ning**), in us. ANNAIBH (**an-niv**), in you. ANNTA (**aoon-ta**), in them.

CHAN 'EIL ANN ACH LEISGEAN, He is nothing but a lazy fellow. Lit. There is not in him but a lazy fellow. LEISGEAN (**lyaysh-gan**) 1. lazy fellow, or person. NA CUIR EARBSA ANNTA. Don't put confidence in them. EARBSA (**erub-sa**) 2. confidence or trust.

Up till now we have used the familiar form CUIR! TOG! but when addressing a person senior to us in age or position we would say CUIRIBH! Put you! TOGAIBH! Lift you! the -IBH or -AIBH being the same as if SIBH were added. Similarly FAG! becomes FAGAIBH! and TRUS! (**troos**) gather! TRUSAIBH! gather you! The -AIBH ending is added where the last vowel of the word is an A, O or U, IBH where it is I.

-AIBH, -IBH both sound -iv CUIRIBH (**koor-iv**), FAGAIBH (**fag-iv**).

NA CUIRIBH EARBSA ANNS AN DUINE SIN! don't put confidence in that man: Note that besides being the polite form CUIRIBH, TOGAIBH, etc., can also refer to more than one person just as YOU in English may do.

Faclair

GAIDHEALTACHD (**ga-el-taCHk**) 2. Highlands.
CEILIDH (**kay-lee**) 2. friendly visit, social evening.
MAR THA, already.
LACHLANN (**laCH-lan**), Lachlan.

AN CEARTUAIR (**ung gyarstar**), presently, at the moment, this moment.
DIREACH (**jee-raCH**) direct, directly.
A BHEAG (**a vek**) any (person or thing): meaning little or few if any.
DE of, off, sharpens if possible the first letter of the next word.
LEASAN (**lay-san**) 1. lesson.
AIR GOIL (**er gull**) boiling.
AIR NEO (**er-nyo**) or else. Stress NEO.
TILG! (**cheel-ig**), throw!
ULLAICH! (**ool-eeCH**) prepare!
FEUR (**fayr**) 1. grass, hay.
LEISGEUL (**lyaysh-kul**) 1. excuse, apology.
THOIR AN AIRE (**hOr an ar-a** with stress on **ar-**) 2. give heed, take care, beware.
MEALL (**mya-ool**) deceive! It can also mean a hill, lump, Class 1.
SLUAGH (**sloo-uGH**) 1. crowd, people, public.
TAIRNEANACH (**tarn-yan-aCH**) 1. thunder.
DEALANACH (**dyal-an-aCH**) 1. lightning.

Gaelic to English

Bha sluagh mor aig a' cheilidh an nochd. An robh Lachlann ann? Cha robh. Chan 'eil e aig an taigh an drasda. Am bheil thu a' tighinn, Eilidh? Tha mi a' tighinn an ceartuair. Tha mi direach a' tighinn. Chaidh am maighstir a mach an ceartuair. Bha i ag radh gun robh flichne ann an diugh. Cuir tuillidh uisge anns a' choire, Aifrig. Cha chuir. Tha gu leoir ann mar tha. Chan 'eil annad ach leigsean. "Cha chuirinn a bheag de earbsa annaibh," thuirt am maighstir an uair nach do dh'ullaich (or nach d'ullaich) na sgoilearan an leasanan. Co th'ann? Tha am posta. Tha an coire air goil. Tog bharr an teine e air neo cha bhi a bheag de uisge ann an uine ghoirid. Chan 'eil a bheag de bhainne againn. An uair a rainig sinn an talla cha robh a bheag ann. Bha tairneanach agus dealanach ann an de. Na tilg paipear air an fheur. Gabh mo leisgeul. Gabhaibh mo leisgeul, athair. Thoir an aire nach tuit thu anns an uisge, Anna. Thoiribh an aire nach meall iad sibh.

Translation

There was a big crowd at the ceilidh to-night. Was Lachlan there? He was not. He is not at home at present. Are you coming, Helen? I am coming this moment (in a jiffy): I am just coming. The master went out just this moment. She was saying that there was sleet to-day. Put more water in the kettle, Effie. I will not. There is plenty in it already. You are just a lazy thing. "I wouldn't put any trust in you," said the master when the scholars didn't prepare their lessons. Who is it? It's the postman. The kettle is boiling. Lift it off the fire (Gaelic, Lift off the fire it) or else there will not be much water in it shortly. We have scarcely any milk. When we reached the hall there were but few there. There was thunder and lightning yesterday. Don't throw paper on the grass. Excuse me (i.e. Take my excuse). Excuse me, father. Take care that you do not fall into the water, Anna. Take care that they do not deceive you.

LESSON 16

The other day, while chatting with MacTavish over a coffee, I asked about our mutual friend Roderick X (RUAIRIDH) (**Rooa-ree**) and my friend replied: " Oh, Roderick is a soldier now." Rory, as we call him for short, has been in a few jobs: this by the way, however. Now as we were speaking in Gaelic, what my friend did say was THA RUAIRIDH 'NA SHAIGHDEAR A NIS. Word for word this would be in English, **Rory is in his soldier now.** It would be wrong to say in Gaelic THA RUAIRIDH SAIGHDEAR A NIS. My friend, who was through the war himself, remarked: " BHA MI 'NAM (AN MO) PHRIOSANACH ANNS A' GHEARMAILT " meaning: **I was a (in my) prisoner in (the) Germany.**

PRIOSANACH (**preesan-aCH**), 1. Prisoner; A' GHEARMAILT (**a yerum-ulch**) 2. (The) Germany.

Now what you have to notice is that **Roderick** and **Soldier** are one and the same person, likewise, **I** and **Prisoner,** when we use this " In " form. Can you remember coming across something like this in the lessons before? For instance, **I am standing at the door** is THA MI 'NAM SHEASAMH AIG AN DORUS. Don't forget that MO, DO and A (His) sharpen if possible the next word, but A (Her), AR, Our; UR, Your; and AN or AM (Their), don't.

Here are a few more examples: THA THU 'NAD CHEALGAIR, You are, Thou art a cheat; CEALGAIR, Class 1. (**cyalug-ir**), A cheat. CHAN 'EIL I 'NA PAISDE A NIS, She is not a child now. PAISDE (**pash-jay**) Class 1 or 2, child. THA NA CARAN 'NAN SOCHAIR MHOR DO'N T-SLUAGH, The cars are a great boon to the public; SOCHAIR (**soCH-ir**), Class 2. Boon; CAR (**kar**) 1. Car.

AM BHEIL SIBH 'NUR BALL DE'N CHOMUNN SEO? Are you a member of this society? BALL (**ba-ool**), Class 1. Member; COMUNN (**kO-mun**), Society; Class 1.

There are two words in Gaelic which you will find very useful in making up little phrases. These are CUIS (**koosh**) and CULAIDH (**kool-ee**). As the last vowel of each is an 'I' they belong, as you will guess, to Class 2. Now we will take the first word CUIS. It means Matter, business, cause or subject of something.

Examples—MILLIDH SIBH A' CHUIS MUR BI SIBH CURAMACH, You will ruin the business unless you are careful. MUR or MUR AN or AM, Unless, If not; CURAMACH (**koora-maCH**), Careful. THA AN SGEIR 'NA CUIS EAGAIL DO NA H-IASGAIREAN, The sunken rock is a source of fear to the fishermen; SGEIR 2. (**skayr**), Skerry or Sunken rock; IASGAIR (**eeask-ir**) 1. fisherman. EAGAL (**ek-al**), 1. Fear; EAGAIL (**ek-il**), Of fear. You will notice that we put an 'I' into EAGAIL. This is the other way, besides using DE, of showing the 'Of' form of the name-word in Gaelic. A few examples are: GEARAN (**gyar-an**), 1. Complaint; GEARAIN (**gyar-ayn**), Of a complaint. MAGADH (**mag-uGH**) 1. Mockery; MAGAIDH (**mag-ee**), Of mockery; MASLADH (**mas-luGH**), 1. Reproach; MASLAIDH (**mas-lee**), Of reproach.

As both CUIS and CULAIDH belong to Class 2, the describing word which comes after them is if possible sharpened. Just as we have CAILEAG MHOR so we have CUIS-MHAGAIDH, CUIS-MHASLAIDH (**vas-lee**) and so on. THA A' CHAILEAG 'NA CUIS-MHASLAIDH DO A MATHAIR, The girl is a cause of reproach to her mother.

CULAIDH means Apparel, suit, object also the material needed to make up anything. CULAIDH AODAICH, Suit of clothes; AODACH (**ood-aCH**), 1. Cloth; also Clothes.

CULAIDH-MHEALLAIDH, A dupe. MEALLADH (**myall-ugh**), 1. Deceit. MEALLAIDH (**myall-ee**), of Deceit.

CULAIDH-GHRAIN, An eye-sore, lit. object of disgust. GRAIN (**gra-een**), 2. Disgust or Loathing.

Note that we did not add an I to GRAIN as there was one there already.

THA AN DEIRCEACH SIN A THA 'NA SHUIDHE AIR A' CHASAN 'NA CHULAIDH-GHRAIN DO'N T-SLUAGH A' DOL SEACHAD. That beggar sitting on the footpath is an eyesore to the public going past.

DEIRCEACH **(jayr-kaCH)** 1. Beggar. DIOL-DEIRCE 1. **(jeel-jayrka)** also used. CASAN, 1. Footpath.

Faclair

PEADAIR **(payd-ir)** 1. Peter.
PIUTHAR **(pyoo-har)** 2. sister.
BANALTRUM **(banal-trum)** 2. nurse.
AM BARAIL **(bar-il)** 2. In opinion, i.e. of the opinion.
CUIDEACHADH **(kooch-aCH-uGH)** 1. help.
DHA **(GHa)** to him.
GNOTHACH **(gro-aCH)** 1. business. Note that GN and CN at the beginning of a word are usually sounded as GR and CR respectively.
GARBH **(gar-uv)**, rough: stormy.
CUIS-MHAGAIDH **(vag-ee)**, Laughing-stock.
NA H-UILE **(na-hoola)** everyone, all.
LEAG **(lyayk)** knock down.
BALLA, 1. wall.
DION **(jee-on)** 1. protection.
CLODHADAIR **(klO-ad-ir)** 1. printer.
ROIMHE SEO **(rOee sho)** formerly.
ROIMH **(rO-ee)** before: sharpens first letter of next word if possible.
GREAS! **(grayss)** haste! hurry! i.e. get a move on (you).
GREAS ORT! Hurry up!
ANMOCH **(ana-moCH)** late in day.
FAODAIDH **(food-ee)** may.
CUIS-GHEARAIN **(yar-ayn)** subject of complaint.
FADALACH **(fad-ul-aCH)** late, dilatory.
CULAIDH-THRUAIS **(kool-ee hru-aysh)** object of pity. Like CUIS, CULAIDH sharpens the next word if possible.
GU **(goo)** to, does not sharpen letters.
SEOLADAIR **(shola-dir)** sailor.

Tha Peadair 'na shaor. Bha mo phiuthar 'na banaltrum. Tha mì am barail gum bheil iad 'nan cealgairean. Bidh an rathad ur 'na shochair do na croitearan. Am bheil fios agaibh gun robh e 'na bhall de 'n chomunn sin an uair a bha e an Canada? Chan 'eil ach tha mi cinnteach gum biodh (bitheadh) e 'na chuideachadh dha anns a' ghnothach aige. Bha e garbh ach tha e 'na la math a nis. Bha an duine bochd 'na chuis-mhagaidh do na h-uile. Tha Iain 'na chleireach agus tha Sine 'na banarach. Na leag am balla sin. Nach 'eil thu a' faicinn gum bheil e 'na dhion do 'n taigh? Nach robh sibh 'nur clodhadairean roimhe seo? Mur greas thu ort bidh sinn fadalach. Mur cuir mi fios gu Mairi roimh Dhi-sathuirn, faodaidh sibh bhi cinnteach nach bi mi a' tighinn idir. Tha a' bhean bhochd sin 'na culaidh-thruais do'n bhaile. Bha e 'na chuis-ghearain aig a' mhaighstir gun robh a' chlann gu tric fadalach anns a' mhaduinn.

Translation

Peter is a joiner. My sister was a nurse. I am of the opinion that they are cheats. The new road will be a boon to the crofters. Do you know that he was a member of that society when he was in Canada? I do not, but I am certain that it would he a help to him in his business. It was stormy but it is a good day now. The poor man was the laughing-stock of all. John is a clerk and Jean is a dairymaid. Don't knock down that wall. Do you not see that it is a protection to the house? Were you not printers formerly (before this)? If you don't hurry up we'll be late. If I don't send word to Mary before Saturday you may be certain that I will not be coming at all. That poor woman is a object of pity to the town. It was the master's complaint that the children were often late in the morning.

LESSON 17

In the last lesson we saw how that a phrase such as He is a sailor would be put in the form He is in his sailor, THA E 'NA SHEOLADAIR. There is, however, another way in which this might have been said in Gaelic and that is by using the word IS (**iss**) instead of THA. Now the word IS attracts to itself the important word in your sentence which would now be written IS SEOLADAIR E, A sailor is he. In other words that is his calling and no other. More commonly, however, Gaelic speakers join the two ways together and say IS E SEOLADAIR A THA ANN, It is a sailor that is in him. In this case the IS E stands for It is, not HE is, and is used in the same way as in the English expression It is he, where 'It' does not refer to any person or thing in particular. Similarly She is a dairymaid would be IS E BANARACH A THA INNTE, It is a dairymaid that is in her ; also John is a joiner would be IS E SAOR A THA AN IAIN.

Note.—Often the AN is doubled and so we hear IS E SAOR A THA ANN AN IAIN. The meaning is just the same.

Having seen how to say He is A joiner, we shall now try He is the joiner and other similar phrases. Notice first of all that we are not starting with It but with He, and so we have IS E AN SAOR. Of course this phrase could also mean, It is the joiner, and so to make the matter perfectly clear we would use the strong form of E which is ESAN (**essan**) meaning He. Thus we would say IS ESAN AN SAOR, He is the joiner. So also IS ESAN AN SAOR A RINN AM BORD, He is the joiner that made the table. IS E AN SAOR A RINN AM BORD is usually taken to mean It is the joiner that made the table.

RINN (**ra-enn** pron. quickly) did, made.

Now while we are at it we may just as well give the strong forms for I, Thou, He, She, etc. These are MISE (**meesha**). TUSA (**toosa**) and THUSA (**oosa**). ESAN (**essan**). ISE (**eesha**). SINNE (**sheen-ya**). SIBHSE (**sheev-sha**). IADSAN (**eead-san**). Use TU or TUSA after IS and its past time which is BU (**boo**) was, were.

IS MISE AM FEAR A THA CIONTACH.

I am the man that is guilty.

CIONTACH (**kyun-taCH**) guilty.

IS MISE A THA SGITH, I am tired. It is I that am tired.

Note.—Notice how the "E" etc. meaning "It" has been dropped after IS in this last phrase. We do not say IS E MISE A THA SGITH. This holds also for TUSA, ISE, etc.

IS IADSAN A BHRIS AN UINNEAG, 'Tis they who broke the window.

So also IS E E A THA FUAR, It is it that is cold i.e. It is indeed cold, becomes IS E (**shay**) A THA FUAR.

Suppose now we want to give the name or relationship of the person in question. All we have to do is to put it in after MI, TU, etc., only using the stronger forms of these where necessary.

IS E DOMHNALL, AN SAOR, He, Donald, is the joiner.

IS I MAIRI, A' CHAILEAG A CHOISINN AN DUAIS. She, Mary, is the girl that won the prize.

DUAIS (**doo-ish**) 2. prize. COISINN! (**koshing**) win!

IS MISE, DOMHNALL BREAC, A THA AIG AN DORUS. It is I, Donald Breck, who am at the door.

IS I MO PHIUTHAR RUNAIR A' CHOMUINN SIN. My sister is secretary of that society.

RUNAIR (**roon-ir**) 1. secretary. BREAC (**breCHk**) speckled, pitted with smallpox; also Class 1, trout.

COMUNN (**kOmun**) 1. society. A' CHOMUINN, of the society.

This last might also have been put IS I MO PHIUTHAR A'S RUNAIR DO'N CHOMUNN SIN. It is she, my sister, that is secretary to that society.

If we put "E" meaning "It" in place of "I" meaning "she" we are merely making a general remark that, my sister happens to be secretary, which you will see is less emphatic.

Note.—IS E can be sounded (**iss ay**) or (**shay**). The "shay" sound is more usual.

Faclair

LURACH (**loor-aCH**) attractive.
UBRAID (**oob-rij**) 2. racket, confusion.
THIG! (**heek**) come!
SUIM (**soo-eem**) 2. heed, respect.
BEATHA (**beh-ha**) 2. life, welcome.
IONNSAICH! (**yoons-eeCH**) learn!
COIMHEAD! (**koy-ad**) look! or looking.
AINM (**en-um**) 1. name.
IOMADH (**eem-a**) many.
ATHARRACHADH (**ar-raCH-uGH**) 1. change. Stress "ar."
SUNND (**soond**) 1. joy, cheerfulness.
DHACHAIDH (**GHaCH-ay**) homewards, also DACHAIDH.
CABHAGACH (**caf-ag-aCH**) in a hurry.
GILLEASBUIG (**geel-es-big**) Archibald. Sound "G" as in "get."
BIORACH (**beer-aCH**) pointed.
TOIL (**tol**) 2. desire.
LAIDIONN (**la-jan**) 2. Latin.
BEAN UASAL (**ben oo-as-al**) 2. lady. Stress the "oo."
CO THA AN SIN (or AN SID)? Who is there, Who's that? AN SID (**sheet**) yonder or there. The "AN" is often dropped in these cases. SID, SUD or SIOD.
CLACHAIR (**klaCH-ir**) 1. mason.

Gaelic to English

Is righ mor e. Is e righ mor a th'ann. Is e caileag lurach a tha innte. Is esan a rinn an ubraid anns an talla. Co tha sid? Tha mise. Chan 'eil ach mise. Tha mi duilich. Is mi a tha duilich. Is iad na canainean a dh'ionnsaich mo nighean anns an sgoil, an Laidionn agus a' Ghaidhlig. Thig a steach. Is e do bheatha. Is iad na h-Americanaich a thog am bata mor ud. Is e clachair math a thog am balla sin. Is math a tha thu a' coimhead. Is cinnteach nach do ghabh e suim do na thuirt sibh. Is e Tormod as ainm do'n bhalach. Is e a tha fliuch an diugh. Is iomadh atharrachadh a chunnaic Domhnall Mor fad a bheatha. Is i Ealasaid a' bhanrigh. Is mor mo shunnd a' tilleadh dhachaidh. Is tu a tha cabhagach. Ma's e do thoil e (or Ma's e ur toil e). Is math sin. Is e sgoilear math a tha an Gilleasbuig. Is e am maireach Di-Sathuirn. Is e beinn ard a th' innte. Is e beinn, cnoc ard biorach. Is e (or i) a' bhean-uasal sin an te a cheannaich na blathan.

Translation

He is a great king. He is a great king. She is an attractive girl. He it is that made the racket in the hall. (We could also say Is esan am fear, etc.) Who is there? I am. Just me or There is not but me. I am sorry. It is I that am sorry. The languages that my daughter learned in school were Latin and Gaelic. Come in. You are welcome. It is the Americans that built that big boat. It is (or was) a good mason that built that wall. You are looking well. (It is well that you, etc.) It is certain (certain is) that he paid (took) no heed to what you said. Norman is the boy's name. (It is Norman that is name to the boy). It is indeed wet to-day. There's many a change or (Many is the change) that big Donald saw during his life. Elizabeth is the queen. Great is my joy returning home (wards). It's you that is in a hurry. If you please: lit. If it's your wish it, the last it meaning the thing that was asked. The "UR" form is used for seniors. That is good (That's fine). Archibald is a good scholar. To-morrow is Saturday. It is a high ben. A ben is a high pointed hill. (This could be put Is e a tha ann am beinn, cnoc ard biorach. Between Is e and a the words An ni, the thing, might be put, but the forms given are evidently shortened). That lady was the person who bought the flowers.

LESSON 18

Consider these two words:—AN DUINE, the man and A' CHLACH the stone. DUINE belongs to Class 1 and CLACH to Class 2. If we put E for AN DUINE and I for A' CHLACH and add to each SEO (**sho**) this, we get E SEO and I SEO both standing for the word. This with the idea of person or thing.

IS E SEO AN DUINE, This is the man.

IS I SEO A' CHLACH, This is the stone, and IS IAD SEO NA DAOINE, CLACHAN, These are the men, stones.

DAOINE (**doon-ya**) men. Stress the "doon".

In the same way E SIN, I SIN stand for That and IAD SIN for Those.

So also E SUD or (SID, SIOD), I SUD, etc., for Yon and IAD SUD, etc., for yon people or things.

IS IAD SUD NA H-IASGAIREAN, Yon men are the fishermen.

Often in speaking we drop the IS E, I, IAD to make the remark more snappy.

SIN AN GILLE A' TIGHINN A NIS, That's the lad coming now.

SUD NA SAIGHDEARAN A' FEITHEAMH RIS A' BHANRIGH. Yon's the soldiers waiting on the queen.

FEITH! (**fay**) wait! FEITHEAMH (**fay-uv**), waiting. RIS (**reesh**) for.

And now to put in question and answer form what we have learned in these two lessons. It is very easy, but you have two things to remember. One is, if the second word of your phrase is E or I or IAD you reply with whichever one of these words you used. Again the IS which should come after AN, CHA, NACH, GUM (which by the way is written GUR) and

MUR, if not, unless, is dropped. GED, although, and MA, if, keep it in. AN E DO PHIUTHAR A THA 'NA SEASAMH THALL AN SIN? Is it your sister that is standing over there? 'SE, It is. CHAN E, It isn't.

THALL (**ha-ool**) over.

NACH I EALASAID A' BHANRIGH? Is not she, Elizabeth, the Queen?

IS I or 'SI. She is. CHAN I, She is not.

MUR E AN DUINE SEO A RINN AM MORT, THA MI FADA AM MEARACHD. If it isn't this man that did the murder, I am far mistaken (far in error).

MORT (**mort** or **morst**) 1. Murder. MEARACHD (**meraCHk**) 2. Mistake, error.

GED IS BEAG E THA E SGAIRTEIL, Though he is small, he is energetic.

SGAIRTEIL (**sgar-chal**) energetic, active.

GED NACH DIREACH E, CHAN 'EIL E CUNNARTACH, Though it is not upright, it is not dangerous. CUNNARTACH (**kooarst-aCH**) dangerous, from CUNNART (**koon-arst**) 1. Danger, risk.

Note here that GED NACH Although not, is the opposite of GED, although, and further that the IS, coming after NACH, was dropped. Phrases like IS BEAG SIN, That is small, IS MATH SIN, That is good are common; but we could also say THA SIN MATH: GED NACH 'EIL E DIREACH and so on.

Suppose now our question turns on a describing-word. Consider these examples.

NACH DONA SIN? Isn't that bad?

Now DONA is a describing-word and our answers would be either SEADH (**shuGH**) meaning Just so! Really, as you say: CHAN EADH (**CHan yuGH**) No indeed!

NACH BOIDHEACH AN DEALBH SIN? Isn't that a beautiful picture?

SEADH, It is indeed. CHAN EADH, It is not.

DEALBH (**ja-luv**) 1. picture.

We might also have replied to the above sentences by saying THA E DONA, GU DEARBH It is bad indeed. CHAN 'EIL E DONA IDIR, It is not bad at all. Similarly for the second sentence by substituting BOIDHEACH for DONA.

AN ALBANNACH E? Is he Scottish? SEADH, That's so. CHAN EADH, not so. ALBANNACH (**Alub-an-aCH**) stress on "AL". Belonging to Scotland or a Scot.

AM MUILEACH E? Is he a Mullman? (i.e. belonging to Mull) SEADH, yes. MUILEACH is here a descriptive word. MUILEACH (**mool-aCH**).

Further Examples :—

THA E AG RADH GUR E LEODHASACH A TH' ANN. HE says he is a Lewisman.

THA E AG RADH GUR LEODHASACH E i.e. GUR (IS) LEODHASACH E.

LEODHASACH (**lyo-as-aCH**) Lewisman, or belonging to Lewis.

Both ways given above are correct but the "TH' ANN" way is the more popular.

THA MI CINNTEACH NACH FIOR E, I am certain that it is not true: or, THA MI CINNTEACH NACH 'EIL E FIOR, which is more common.

Faclair

SGITHEANACH (**skee-an-aCH**) Skyeman.
ILEACH (**ee-laCH**) Islayman.
FALLAIN (**fal-ayn**) healthy.
SEALLADH (**shall-uGH**) 1. view, sight, eyesight.
FOGHAR (**fOur**) 1. autumn, harvest.
MOTHAICH! (**mo-eeCH**), perceive! feel! notice!
COIGREACH (**kOeeg-raCH**) 1. foreigner, stranger.
GOIRT (**gorst**) painful, sore.
A MHAIN (**a van**), only.
TEANN (**cha-oon**) tight.
BRUTHAINNEACH (**broo-hin-yaCH**), sultry, close, stuffy.
GU DEARBH (**jer-uv**) indeed.
FARPUISEACH (**far-push-aCH**) 1. competitor.
FARPUISICH (**far-push-eeCH**) competitors.
Often CO-FHARPUISEACH, etc. FARPUIS (**far-push**) 2. competition; also CO-FHARPUIS.

UILE (**oola**) all.
TOGAIL (**tOk-al**) 2. building.
SEAN (**shen**) old. Spelt SEANN before a name-word beginning with D, N, T, L, S, R: all others SEAN.
CO DHIUBH (**kO yoo**) Which of them, however, whether.
TEAS (**chayss**) 1. heat.
AN DA CHUID (**CHooj**) both.
DIULT! (**joolt**) refuse!
COBHAIR (**kO-er**) 2. help.
NEACH SAM BITH (**nyeCH sam be**) anyone at all.
BREITHEAMH (**bray-uv**) 1. judge, umpire, referee.
RIS, with.
CEUD (**kayd**) first.
BEARTACH (**byarst-aCH**) rich.
FIALAIDH (**feeal-ee**) generous, hospitable.
AN meaning "in" is often doubled, thus ANN AN i.e. "in in"; or ANN AM before words beginning with B, F, M, P. (See Lesson 17 Note).

Gaelic to English

An e Sgitheanach a bh' ann? Chan e, ach Ileach. Ma's fuar e, tha e fallain. Nach iad sin na farpuisich a tha a' tighinn an rathad seo? Is iad (or Is iad a th'ann). An e sin uile? Is e. An e sin uile e? 'Se. Chan e. Nach e a tha bruthainneach an diugh? Is e gu dearbh. Nach don an gnothach sin? Seadh, tha e dona. Am Muileach e? Chan eadh, ach Ileach. An i sud a' bhean uasal a chaill a rathad air a' bheinn? Chan i idir, chan 'eil fios agam co i. Ged nach mor e, tha e laidir. Nach boidheach an sealladh e anns an fhoghar? Seadh, tha e gle bhoidheach. Co dhiubh is iad na cuileagan no an teas a tha a' cur dragh oirbh? Is e an teas. An da chuid. Nach e seann togail a th' innte? Chan e, chan 'eil i cho sean idir. Co i an te sin a tha a' bruidhinn ris a' bhreitheamh? 'S i sin a' chaileag a choisinn a' cheud duais an diugh. Mhothaich mi gur e coigreach a bh'ann. An e mise? Is tusa. Cha tusa. Is e. Chan e. Is e a tha ann am MacNeill duine nach diultadh cobhair do neach sam bith. Is e a' bhanrigh a th'ann. Is i (ise) a' bhanrigh. Is e banrigh a th'innte.

Translation

Was he a Skyeman? No, but an Islayman. If it is cold, it is healthy. Aren't those the competitors that are coming this way? They are. Is that all? It is. Is that it all? It is. It isn't. Isn't it sultry to-day? It is indeed. Isn't that a bad business? That's so, it is bad. Is he a Mullman? No, but an Islayman. Is yon (or that) the lady that lost her way on the mountain? Not at all, I don't know who she is. Though he is not big, he is strong. Isn't it a beautiful sight in the autumn? Yes indeed, it is very beautiful. Whether is it the flies or the heat that is troubling you? It is the heat. Both. Is it not an old building? No, it is not so old at all. Who is that person that is talking to the judge? That is the girl that won the first prize to-day. I noticed that he was a foreigner. Is it I? It's you. It isn't you. It is. It isn't. MacNeill is (It is it that is in M) a man that would not refuse help to anyone. It is the queen. She is the queen. She is a queen.

LESSON 19

There is one little word in Gaelic which would seem to have collected in its progress quite a wide variety of meaning. It is RI or RIS which means With, at, as, towards, out, etc. Its use is best learned from examples.

BHA E A' BRUIDHINN RIS AN DUINE SIN. He was speaking with that man.

THA MO MHAC RI SAORSAINNEACHD. My son is employed as a carpenter or at carpentry.

THA DOMHNALL CHO CRUAIDH RIS AN DARACH. Donald is as hard (unyielding) as the oak.

BHA AN GILLE COLTACH RI A ATHAIR. The boy was like (similar to) his father.

CUIR A' GHLOINE RI DO SHUIL. Put the glass to your eye.

CHUIR SINN NA CAORAICH RIS A' MHONADH. We put (drove) the sheep towards the hill.

SAORSAINNEACHD (**soors-in-yeCHk**) 2. joinery, carpentry. DARACH 1. oak. GLOINE (**glon-ya**) 2. (also 1) glass. MONADH (**mon-uGH**) 1. hill pasture. Use RIS instead of RI before AN (A'), NA all meaning "The".

RI also joins with MI, TU, etc., just as LE did with these words. Further, and this is a point we have not touched on before, they can all, like MI-SE, TU-SA have a strong form. We shall now show the ordinary and strong forms for RI and this will do for all the others.

RIUM-SA (**room-sa**) at me. RIUT-SA (**root-sa**) at thee. RIS-SAN (**reesh-san**) at him, it. RITHE-SE (**reeha-sha**) at her, it. RUINN-NE (**roon-ya**) at us. RUIBHSE (**roov-sha**) at you. RIU-SAN (**roo-san**) at them. FHEIN (**hayn**) meaning self could also have been used instead of these endings. THA MI A' BRUIDHINN RIUTSA or RIUT FHEIN.

It is with your (or yourself) I am speaking.

In our past lessons we have come across quite a number of small words such as AIR, on, ANNS, in, AIG, at, LEIS, with, and so on. Now when we use them along with the question form of the action-word they translate very neatly the English terms On whom, on which, In whom, in which, etc. A few examples will make this clear.

AM BHEIL E A' FALBH? Is he going away?

IS MISE AN DUINE LEIM AM BHEIL E A' FALBH. I am the man with whom he is going away.

AM BI E A' FALBH AN DIUGH? Will he be going off to-day?

IS MISE AN DUINE LEIS AM BI E A' FALBH AN DIUGH. I am the man with whom he will be going off to-day.

AN CUIR E AN SIOL? Will he sow the seed?

THREABH AN TUATHANACH AN TALAMH ANNS AN CUIR E AN SIOL. The farmer ploughed the land in which he will sow the seed.

TREABH! (**trO**) plough! THREABH (**hrO**) ploughed.

TALAMH (**tal-uv**) 1. land, earth. SIOL (**sheeul**) 1. seed. CUIR! (**koor**) Sow! put!

Now try past time.

BHUAIL E AN CU. He struck the dog. AN DO BHUAIL E AN CU? Did he strike the dog?

C' AIT' AM BHEIL AM BATA LEIS AN DO BHUAIL E AN CU? Where is the stick with which he struck the dog?

THUIT AN DEILE AIR AN ROBH IAD 'NAN SEASAMH. The plank on which they were standing fell.

DEILE (**jay-la**) 2. plank.

THA OBAIR-UISGE ANNS A' GHLEANN GUS AN. DO CHOISICH IAD. There is a water-works in the glen to which they walked. GUS (**goos**) to which GLEANN (**glya-oon**) 1. glen.

BHRIS E A' GHLOINE AS AN DO DH'OL (AN D'OL short form) E AM FION. He broke the glass out of which he drank the wine.

Faclair

CO RIS (**kO reesh**)? Who with or with whom?

AGHAIDH (**uGHY**) 2. face.

LEIG! (**lyayg**) let! allow!

LEIGEIL (**lyay-gal**) letting, allowing.

LEIG RIS, show, prove.

TAIC (**teCHk**) 2. support.

LEIG MI MO THAIC RI, I let my support at, leaned.

AN TAIC RI, against.

RURAICH! (**roo-reeCH**) rummage!

RURACH (**roo-raCH**) rummaging.

CISTE (**keest-ya**) 2. chest.

AIR SON, for.

RUD AIR CHOR-EIGINN (**CHor-ayking**) something or other.

CIOD? (**kut**) what? Also De? (**jay**).

FUAIGH! (**foo-ay**) sew!

FUAIGHEAL (**foo-yal**) sewing.

FIGH! (**fee**) knit! weave!

FIGHEADH (**fee-yuGH**) knitting, weaving.

STOCAINN-EAN (**stoCHk-ing, stoCHkin-yan**) stocking-s 2.

DEANADACH (**jayn-ad-aCH**) industrious.

LEISG (**lyayshk**) 2. laziness.

GRIAN (**greean**) 2. sun.
AIREAMH (**a-riv**) 1. number.
AM BHEIL CUIMHNE AGAD AIR, Is remembrance at you on? Do you remember?
CUIMHNE (**kooin-ya**) 2. memory, remembrance.
NI (**nyee**) 1. thing.
MU (**moo**) about.
A CHIALL! (**CHeeal**) Dear me!
DEIGH (**jay**) 2. ice.
TREIS (**tresh**) 2. while.
CNAP (**krap**) 1. lump.
STOB (**stob**) 1. post.
OLC (**olk**) bad.
AON (**oon**) one, same.

Gaelic to English

Co ris a tha e a' bruidhinn? Chuir e a aghaidh ris a' bhalla. Leig i a taic ris an stob. Ciod e (or De) a tha an droch bhalach ris a nis? Tha e a' rurach anns a' chiste air son rud air chor-eiginn. Ciod e a ("a" usually omitted) tha an te bheag ris? Tha i ri fuaigheal agus tha a piuthar mhor ri figheadh stocainnean air son Iain. Nach iad na caileagan deanadach! Is olc an rud an leisg. Nach boidheach an sealladh an uair a tha a' ghrian ris! Seadh, tha e gle bhoidheach. Tha seo a' leigeil ris gum bheil an drochaid sin gle chunnartach. Chuir iad coig eile ris an aireamh. Am bheil cuimhne agaibh air an duine uasal ris an do bhruidhinn sibh anns an taigh-cafe an de? Tha, ach chan 'eil cuimhne agam air an ni mu'n robh sinn a' briudhinn. A chiall! tha do lamhan cho fuar ri cnap deigh. Bha iad aig an aon sgoil ruinn-ne. Ciod e thachair do'n duine bho'n do cheannaich mi an car? Dh'fhag e am baile o chionn treis.

Translation

With whom is he speaking? He turned (put) his face to the wall. She leaned against the post. What's the bad lad up to (at) now? He is rummaging in the chest for something or other. What's the little one at? She is (busy) at sewing and her big sister is busy knitting stockings for Iain. Aren't they the industrious girls! Laziness is a bad thing (lit. Bad is the thing, the laziness). Isn't the view beautiful when the sun is out! Yes indeed, it is very beautiful. This shows that that bridge is very dangerous. They added (put) five others to the number. Do you remember (Is remembrance at you on) the gentleman with whom you spoke in the coffee-house yesterday? I do, but I don't remember the matter about which we were speaking (or spoke). Dear me! your hands are as cold as a lump of ice. They were at the same school as we. What happened to the man from whom I bought the car? He left the town a short time ago.

LESSON 20

We have seen how a phrase such as It was a beautiful sight, might be put into Gaelic as BHA E 'NA SHEALLADH BOIDHEACH or IS E SEALLADH BOIDHEACH A BH' ANN.

Now this could be put in still another way by using BU (**boo**) which is the past time of IS. BU sharpens the first letter of the following word if possible and drops its "U" before a vowel. Thus we have BU SHEALLADH BOIDHEACH E, It was a beautiful sight or view.

If we wanted to stress the fact of its being beautiful we might say BU BHOIDHEACH AN SEALLADH E. As you will notice, we have taken the descriptive word "BOIDHEACH" away from SEALLADH and placed it next to BU for emphasis.

Here are a few examples of the use of BU.

B'E OIDHCHE GHARBH A BH'ANN, It was a rough night.

B'E IAIN A B'AINM DO'N BHALACH, It was Iain that was name to the boy: i.e. Iain was the name of the boy.

BU MHOR AM MILLEADH A RINN NA SAIGHDEARAN AIR A' BHAILE. Great was the damage that the soldiers did on the town.

MILLEADH (**meel-yuGH**) 1. damage.

AM B'E NA GILLEAN A MHILL NA BLATHAN? Was it the boys that destroyed the flowers? B'E, It was. CHA B'E, It was not. THA MI CINNTEACH NACH B'E, I am certain that it was not. We could also have used IS instead of BU (B'E) in these last four phrases and IAD instead of E in the last, in both question and reply. Notice how we answer when the describing word comes next to BU in a question.

NACH BU CHUNNARTACH AN CLUICH A BHI SNAMH AGUS AN LAN A' DOL A MACH? Was it not a dangerous game to be swimming and the tide going out? B'EADH (**byuGH**) It was. CHA B'EADH, It was not. We could also have said, BU CHUNNARTACH GU DEARBH, It was dangerous indeed, or CHA BU CHUNNARTACH IDIR, It was not at all; also BHA E CUNNARTACH, CHA ROBH E CUNNARTACH.

LAN (lan) 1. tide; also meaning "full" or "fully." LAN CHEART, fully right. CLUICH (**kloo-eeCH**) 1. game.

In a previous lesson we dealt with such phrases as THA LA MATH ANN; It is a fine day: AN TU A TH'ANN? Is it you? BHA SLUAGH MOR ANN, There was a big crowd present. Now we can use ANN along with IS and BU to give emphasis to what we are saying. Thus, THA E AG OBAIR ANNS A' BHAILE A NIS, He is working in the town now, might also be put IS ANN ANNS A' BHAILE A THA E AG OBAIR A NIS: It is in the town that he is working now. The IS ANN equals "really" or "indeed" in such phrases.

IS ANN AIGE A THA AN T-AIRGIOD, He it is that has the money.

IS ANN A' COISEACHD A BHA E, It was walking that he was.

AN ANN AN SEO A THACHAIR AN TUBAIST? Is it here that the accident happened? TUBAIST (**toob-isht**) 2. accident. CHAN ANN, It is not. IS ANN, It is. CHUALA MI GUR ANN AN SEO A THACHAIR AN TUBAIST, I heard that it is here that the accident happened. Notice that GUN is changed to GUR and that the IS has been dropped. Now a few examples with B'ANN.

B'ANN MAR SIN A THACHAIR(E), It was thus that it happened. E after THACHAIR usually omitted.

NACH B'ANN ANNS A' CHOGADH A CHAILL E A BHEATHA? Was it not in the war that he lost his life? B'ANN. It was. CHA B'ANN. It was not.

CHA does not sharpen BU: also CHA and BU do not sharpen a D or a T.

COGADH (**kog-uGH**) 1. war. CHAILL (**CHa-eel**) lost, from CAILL! (**ka-eel**) lose!

THUIG MUINNTIR AN AITE NACH B'ANN MAR CHARAID A THAINIG E. The people of the place understood that it was not as a friend that he came.

MUINNTIR (**mooin-cheer**) 2. people, inhabitants, relations. MAR, as, sharpens next word if possible.

Faclair

GNIOMH (**greev**) 1. deed.
OILLTEIL (**oyl-chayl**), shocking, terrifying.
MIANN (**me-unn**) 1. desire, intention.
BRONACH (**bron-aCH**), sad.
CRUINNICH! (**kroon-yeeCH**) gather!
CUIDEACHD (**kooch-aCHk**) 2. company.
BEUD (**bayd**) 1. pity, harm.
CAILLTE (**kal-chay**) lost.
AN AITE (**un acha**) instead (of).
SEANMHAIR (**shenuv-er**) 2. grandmother.
TOILEACHAS (**tolaCH-as**) 1. pleasure.
SGEUL (**skayl**) 1. story, news.
SGEULACHD (**skayl-aCHk**) 2. tale, story (old or new).
AINMEIL (**enum-il**) famous.
SPAIRN (**sparn**) 2. great exertion.

Gaelic to English

B'e mo bharail nach tigeadh iad. B'iad sin na laithean cruaidh. Cha b'fhada gus an robh e air ais. B'i Banrigh Ealasaid a rinn an gniomh oillteil sin. Cha bu tric a chaidh iad an rathad sin. B'e mo mhainn an uair a bha mi 'nam bhalach a bhi 'nam sheoladair. Bu bhronach a' chuideachd a chruinnich anns a' ghleann. Bu mhor am beud gun robh iad cho anmoch. Nam b'e an diugh an de, cha bhithinn-sa mar a tha mi. Mur b'e gun robh e an sud, bhiomaid uile caillte.

Is ann ag iasgach a tha iad, an aite a bhi anns an sgoil. An ann anns a' choille a tha a' chlann? Chan ann, ach anns a' phairc. Nach ann aige a tha fios. Is ann gu dearbh. Nach ann a nis a tha e gle bheartach? Is ann an de a rainig iad. Tha fios againn gur ann le Iain a tha an leabhar agus nach ann le Seumas. B' ann bho mo sheanmhair a fhuair mi am fainne. Cha b'ann le toileachas a chuala sinn an sgeul. Nach bu trom e? B'eadh, gu dearbh. Cha b'eadh idir. Tha e cinnteach nach b'ann gun spairn a dh'fhas e cho ainmeil.

Translation

It was my opinion that they would not come. Those were the hard days. It was not long till he was back. It was Queen Elizabeth that did that shocking deed. It wasn't often that they went that way. It was my desire when I was a boy to be a sailor. It was a sorrowful company that gathered in the glen. It was a great pity that they were so late. If to-day were yesterday, I should not be as I am. Had he not been there (lit. If it were not that he was there) we should all have been lost.

It is fishing that they are, instead of being in school. Is it in the wood that the children are? No, but in the park. Isn't it he that knows? It is indeed. Isn't he very rich now? It is (or was) yesterday that they arrived. We know that the book belongs to Iain and not to James. It was from my grandmother that I got the ring. It wasn't with pleasure that we heard the news. Was it not heavy? It was indeed. It wasn't at all. It is certain that it was not without a hard struggle that he became so famous.

VOCABULARY

FACLAIR

Bracketed forms are to be understood as follows:—

Rathad (rathaid, rathaidean), a road (of a road, roads).
Bris (briseadh), break, breaking.
Cobhair (cobhrach) 2. help, of help.

A

A, his or her.
A, out of. See AS.
A, that: referring to person or thing.
Abhainn (aibhne, aibhnichean) 2. river.
A bheag, few if any, very little.
Ach, but.
A chiall! O dear!
A chionn, because.
Acras (acrais) 1. hunger.
Ad (aide, adan) 2. hat.
A dhith, lacking, a-wanting, required.
Aghaidh (aghaidh, aghaidhean) 2. face.
Agus, and.
A h-uile, every: but na h-uile, all.
Aifrig, 2. Euphemia.
Aig, at.
Aimsir (aimsire, aimsirean) 2. time, weather, season.
Ainm (ainme, ainmean) 1. name.
Ainmeil, famous.
Air, on; also on him or it.
Air ais, back.
Air ball, on the spot, immediately.
Air choireigin, somehow or other.
Air cuairt, on a visit.
Aireamh (aireimh) 2. amount, quantity, number.
Air falbh, off, away.
Airgiod (airgid) 1. money, silver.
Air goil, boiling.
Air neo, otherwise.
Air son, for the sake of, because.
Aite (aite, aiteachan) 1. place.
Aithne (aithne) 2. knowledge, acquaintance.
Aitidh, damp.
Alba (Alba) 2. Scotland.
Alasdair, 1. Alexander.
A mach, out (motion).
A mhain, only.
Am maireach, to-morrow.
An, an t-, the.
An, in; also found Ann an (am).
An aire, 2. attention, heed.
An aite, instead of.
An ceartuair, in a moment or just a moment ago.
An da chuid, both.
An de, yesterday.
An d' fhuair sibh? did you get or find?
An diugh, to-day.
An drasda, presently, at present.
An earar, the day after to-morrow.
A nis, now.
Anmoch, late.
Ann, in him or it or in existence.
Anna, Anna.
An nochd, to-night.
Anns an, in the.
An raoir, last-night.
An seo, here.
An sin, there, then.
An sud, yonder.
An uair a, when.
An uiridh, last year.
Aodach (aodaich, aodaichean) 1. cloth, clothes.
Aoigheachd, 2. entertainment, lodging.

Aon, one, same.
Aonta (aonta, aontaichean) 1. lease.
Aran (arain) 1. bread.
Ard, high, tall.
A rithist (or a ris), again.
Arm (airm, armailtean) 1. army.
As, out of, from.
A steach, in (motion).
Athair (athar, athraichean) 1. father.
Atharrachadh, 1. change, alteration.

B

Baile (baile, bailtean) 1. town.
Bainne, 1. milk.
Bainne goirt, sour milk.
Balach (balaich, balaich) 1. boy.
Ball (buill, buill) 1. member.
Balla (balla, ballachan) 1. wall.
Ban, fair, white.
Banais (bainnse, bainnsean) 2. wedding.
Banaltrum (banaltruim, banaltruimean) 2. nurse.
Banarach (banaraich, banaraich) 2. dairymaid.
Banrigh (banrigh, banrighean) 2. queen.
Barail (baralach, baralaichean) 2. opinion.
Bata (bata, bataichean) 1. boat.
Beag, small.
Bean (mna, mnathan) 2. woman.
Bean an taighe, 2. housewife.
Bean uasal, 2. lady.
Beartach, rich.
Beatha (beatha, beathannan 2. life. Used with Mo, do etc. to mean Welcome!
Beinn (beinne, beanntan) 2. mountain.
Beud (beud, beudan) 1. pity, harm.
Beurla, 2. English: also Beurla Shasunnach.
Bho, from.
Bharr, off.
Bi, be. A bhi to be.
Binn, melodious.
Biorach, pointed.
Blath, warm.
Bo (ba or boin, ba) 2. cow.
Bochd, poor.
Bodach (bodaich, bodaich) 1. old man.
Boidheach, beautiful, pretty.
Bodhar, deaf.
Boirionnach (boirionnaich, boirionnaich) 1. woman.
Bonnach (bonnaich, bonnaich) 1. cake.
Bord (buird, buird) 1. table.
Braiste (braiste, braistean) 2. brooch.
Bratach (brataich, brataichean) 2. flag.
Breac (bric, bric) 1. trout: also speckled.
Breitheamh (breitheimh, breitheamhan) 1. judge.
Briagh, fine; also Breagh.
Bris (briseadh) break.
Briste, broken.
Brog (broige, brogan) 2. shoe.
Bron (broin) 1. sorrow.
Bronach, sorrowful.
Bruich (bruich) boil.
Bruidhinn (bruidhinn) speak.
Bruthainneach, sultry, close.
Buail (bualadh) strike.
Buth (butha, buithean) 1. shop.

C

Cabhag (cabhaige) 2. haste.
Cabhagach, hurried, in haste.
Caidil (cadal) sleep.
Caileag (caileige, caileagan) 2. little girl, lassie.
Caill (call) lose.
Caillte, lost.
Cailleach (cailliche, cailleachan) 2. old woman.
Cais or **Caise** (caise, caisean) 1. cheese.
C'aite, where?

Canain (canaine, canainean) 2. language.
Caol, thin, narrow.
Caora (caorach, caoraich) 2. sheep.
Car, somewhat.
Car (cair, caran or caraichean) 1. car.
Caraid (caraid, cairdean) 1. male friend.
C'ar son, why?
Cas, steep.
Cas (coise, casan) 2. foot.
Casan (casain, casanan) 1. foot-path.
Cat (cait, cait) 1. cat.
Cathair (cathrach, cathraichean) 2. chair; also city.
Catriona, 2. Catherine.
Cealgair (cealgair, cealgairean) 1. cheat, rogue.
Ceann (cinn, cinn) 1. head.
Ceannaich (ceannach) buy.
Ceapaire (ceapaire, ceapairean) 1. sandwich.
Cearc (circe, cearcan) 2. hen.
Ceilidh (ceilidh, ceilidhean) 2. ceilidh, social visit.
Ceo (ceo, ceothan) 1. mist.
Ceol (ciuil) 1. music.
Ceud, first; also hundred.
Ceum (ceim, ceuman) 1. step.
Chaidh, went.
Chuala, heard.
Chunnaic, saw.
Ciobair (ciobair, ciobairean) 1. shepherd.
Cinnteach, sure, certain.
Ciod, what?
Cionntach, guilty.
Ciste (ciste, cistean) 2. chest.
Ciurr (ciurradh) hurt.
Clach (cloiche, clachan) 2. stone.
Clachair (clachair, clachairean) 1. mason.
Clann (cloinne) 2. children.
Cleireach (cleirich, cleirich) 1. clerk.
Clodhadair (clodhadair, clodhad-airean) 1. printer.
Cluich (cluiche, cluichean) 1. game.
Cluich (cluich) play, as game or instrument.
Cnap (cnaip, cnapan) 1. lump, button.
Co, who?
Cobhair (cobhrach) 2. help.
Co dhiubh, at any rate, whether.
Cogadh (cogaidh, cogaidhean) 1. war.
Coig, five.
Coigreach (coigrich, coigrich) 1. stranger.
Coileach (coilich, coilich) 1. cock.
Coille (coille, coilltean) 2. wood.
Coimhead (coimhead) observe, look at.
Coinnich (coinneachadh) meet.
Coire (coire, coireachan) 1. kettle.
Coire (coire, coireannan) 2. fault.
Coireach, blameable, to blame.
Coisich (coiseachd) walk.
Coisinn (cosnadh) win, earn.
Coltach, like or likely.
Coma, indifferent, all the same.
Comunn (comuinn, comuinn) 1. society.
Copan (copain, copanan) 1. cup.
Co ris, with whom?
Cota (cota, cotaichean) 1. coat.
Craobh (craoibhe, craobhan) 2. tree.
Creag (creige, creagan) 2. rock.
Creid (creidsinn) believe, think.
Crodh (cruidh) 1. cattle.
Croitear (croiteir, croitearan) 1. crofter.
Cruaidh, hard.
Crosda, ill-natured.
Cruinnich (cruinneachadh) gather.
Cu (coin, coin) 1. dog.
Cuid (codach, codaichean) 2. share, part.
Cuideachadh (cuideachaidh) 1. help.
Cuideachd (cuideachd, cuideachd-an) 2. company.
Cuideachd, also.
Cuidich (cuideachadh) help.

Cuileag (cuileige, cuileagan) 2. fly.
Cuimhne (cuimhne) 2. memory.
C'uine, when?
Cuir (cur) put, plant.
Cuis (cuise, cuisean) 2. matter, affair.
Cuis-ghearain, matter of complaint.
Cul (cuil, cuiltean) 1. back, hinder part.
Culaidh (culaidh, culaidhean) 2. object; also apparel.
Culaidh-thruais, object of pity.
Cunnart (cunnairt, cunnartan) 1. danger, risk.
Cunnartach, dangerous, risky.
Cum (cumail) hold, keep.
Curamach, careful.

D

Da, two.
Dachaidh (dachaidh, dachaidhean) 2. home.
Dachaidh or **Dhachaidh,** homewards.
Daonnan, always.
Darach (daraich, daraich) 1. oak-tree.
De, what?
De, off, cf.
Dealanach (dealanaich) 1. lightning-flash.
Dean (deanamh) do, make.
Dean cabhag! hurry up! make haste!
Deanadach, diligent, industrious.
Deas, ready.
Deasaich (deasachadh) prepare, make ready.
Deigh (deighe, deighean) 2. ice.
Deile (deilidh, deileachan 2. plank.
Deirceach (deircich, deircich) 1. beggar; also Diol deirce.
Deise (deise, deiseachan) 2. suit of clothes.
Deorsa, 1. George.
Dha, to him, to it.
Di-luain, 1. Monday.
Di-Sathuirn, 1. Saturday.
Direach, straight; also exactly.
Dirich (direadh) climb.
Diult (diultadh) refuse.
Dion (dionadh) protect, defend.
Diura, Jura.
Dochann (dochainn, dochannan) 1. damage, injury.
Do, to.
Dol, going.
Domhnall (Domhnaill) 1. Donald.
Dona, bad.
Donn, brown.
Dorus (doruis, dorsan) 1. door.
Dorus-cuil, 1. back-door.
Dragh (dragha) 1. trouble, annoyance.
Drochaid (drochaide, drochaidean) 2. bridge.
Druim (droma, dromannan) 1. back; also ridge of hill.
Duais (duaise, duaisean) 2. prize, reward.
Dubh, black.
Duilich, sorry, difficult.
Duilleag (duilleige, duilleagan) 2. leaf.
Duin (dunadh) shut.
Duine (duine, daoine) 1. man, person.
Duine uasal, gentleman.
Duthaich (duthcha, duthchannan) 2. country.

E

Each (eich, eich) 1. horse.
Eadh, used with Is and Bu, meaning It.
Eagal (eagail) 1. fear.
Eaglais (eaglaise, eaglaisean) 2. church.
Ealasaid, 2. Elizabeth.
Earbsa (earbsa), 2. trust, confidence.
Eilidh, 2. Helen.
Eire (Eireann) 2. Ireland.
Eirich (eirigh) rise.
Eoghann (Eoghainn) Ewen.
Eolach, acquainted; also intelligent.
Esan, he (emphatic form).

F

Facal (facail, facail or faclan) 1. word.
Faclair (faclair, faclairean) 1. vocabulary, dictionary.
Fada, long.
Fad an latha, during the day.
Fadalach, late, tedious, dilatory.
Fag (fagail) leave.
Faicinn, seeing.
Fainne (fainne, fainneachan) 1. ring.
Falbh as in Air falbh, away, off. Falbh also means going.
Fallan (or fallain) sound, healthy.
Fan (fantuinn) stay.
Faod, may, can. Faodaidh mi, I may.
Faotainn, getting, finding.
Far, where, in the place that.
Farpuis (farpuise, farpuisean) 2. contest, competition: also found as Co-fharpuis.
Farpuiseach (farpuisich, farpuisich) 1. competitor: also Co-fharpuiseach.
Fasach (fasaich, fasaichean) 1. desert.
Feadhainn (feadhna) 2. group of persons or things, some.
Fear (fir, fir) 1. man: also an object belonging to Class 1.
Fear-labhairt, 1. speaker, spokesman.
Fear-lagha, 1. lawyer.
Fear-tagraidh, 1. barrister.
Fearg (feirge) 2. anger.
Feasgar (feasgair, feasgair or feasgairean) 1. evening.
Feith (feitheamh) wait.
Feum (feuma) 1. need. Feumaidh mi, I need or must.
Feur (feoir) 1. grass, hay.
Fhathast, yet.
Fhuair, got, found.
Fialaidh, generous, hospitable.
Figh (figheadh) weave, knit.
Fiodh (fiodha) 1. wood, timber.
Fion (fiona) 1. wine.
Fios (fiosa) 1. knowledge, information.
Flichne, 1. sleet.
Fliuch, wet.
Fo, under.
Foghar (foghair) 1. harvest, autumn.
Fosgail (fosgladh) open. Fosgailte, opened, open.
Frangach, French, Frenchman.
Fraoch (fraoich) 1. heather.
Fras (froise, frasan) 2. shower.
Frasach, showery.
Freagair (freagradh) answer.
Freagairt (freagairt, freagairtean) 2. answer.
Fuachd (fuachd, fuachdan) 1. or 2. cold, coldness.
Fuaigh (fuaigheal) sew.
Fuar, cold.
Fuaraidh, damp, chilly.

G

Gabh (gabhail) take; also go.
Gabh air, beat.
Gabh sraid, take a walk.
Gaidhealtachd, 2. Highlands.
Gaidhlig, 2. Gaelic.
Gairdean (gairdein, gairdeanan) 1. arm.
Gairdeanach, having arms.
Gann, scarce.
Gaoth (gaoithe, gaoithean) 2. wind.
Garbh, rough, coarse.
Gasda, fine, excellent.
Geal, bright.
Geall (gealladh) promise.
Ged, although.
Gearan (gearain, gearanan) 1. complaint.
Gearan (gearain) complain.
Gearmailt (Gearmailte) 2. Germany: used as A' Ghearmailt, Germany.
Gearr, short.
Gearr (gearradh) cut.
Gille (gille, gillean) 1. boy.
Gilleasbuig, Gillespie, Archibald.

Giulain (giulan) carry.
Glan, clean.
Glas, grey; also green applied to hills, trees.
Glaschu, Glasgow.
Gleann (glinne, gleanntan) 1. glen.
Gleidh (gleidheil) keep.
Gloine (gloine, gloineachan) 1. or 2. glass.
Gniomh (gniomha, gniomharran) 1. deed.
Gnothach (gnothaich, gnothaichean) 1. business, affair.
Goirid, short.
Goirt, sore, painful; also bitter, sour.
Goirtich (goirteachadh) hurt.
Gorm, blue.
Gradh (graidh) 1. love.
Grain (graine or grain) 2. disgust.
Greas (greasadh) hurry.
Greusaiche (greusaiche, greusaichean) 1. shoemaker.
Grian (greine) 2. sun.
Grianaig, 2. Greenock.
Grinn, handsome, elegant.
Gu, to; also equals -ly in English as below.
Gu brath, for ever.
Gu cinnteach, certainly.
Gu dearbh, indeed.
Gu dona, badly.
Gu glan, cleanly.
Gu h-aithghearr, shortly.
Gu leoir, enough.
Gu math, well.
Gu pailt, plentifully.
Gu toileach, willingly.
Gu tric, often.
Gu trom, heavily.
Gun, Gum, that.
Gun tig, that shall come.
Gus, until.

I

Iain, 1. John.
Iarr (iarraidh) ask, request, look for.
Iasg (eisg) 1. fish.
Iasgaich (iasgach) fish.
Iasgair (iasgair, iasgairean) 1. fisherman.
Idir, at all.
Ileach (Ilich, Ilich) 1. Islayman; also belonging to Islay.
Im (ime) 1. butter.
Inbhir Air, Air.
Inbhir Nis, Inverness.
Innis (innseadh or innse) tell, say, relate.
Iomadh, many.
Iomain (iomain) drive.
Iomair (iomradh) row.
Ionnsaich (ionnsachadh) learn.
Ith (itheadh) eat.

L

La (la, laithean) 1. day.
Lachlann (Lachlainn) 1. Lachlan.
Laidionn (Laidinn) 2. Latin.
Laidir, strong.
Laigh (laighe) lie down.
Lamh (laimhe, lamhan) 2. hand.
Lan, full, completely.
Lan (lain, lain) 1. tide.
Laomuinn, Lomond.
Lar (lair) 1. ground.
Le, leis, with.
Leabag (leabaige, leabagan) 2. flounder.
Leabaidh (leapa, leapaichean) 2. bed.
Leabhar (leabhair, leabhraichean) 1. book.
Leag (leagadh), knock down, lay.
Leasan (leasain, leasain) 1. lesson.
Leig (leigeil) let, allow.
Leisg, lazy.
Leisgean (leisgein, leisgeanan) 1. lazy person.
Leisgeul (leisgeil, leisgeulan) 1. excuse, apology.
Lighiche (leigh, lighichean) 1. medical man, physician.
Leodhasach (Leodhasaich, Leodhasaich) 1. Lewisman.
Lion (lionadh) fill.

Litir (litreach, litreachan) 2. letter.
Locair (locair, locraichean) 2. carpenter's plane ; also Locar 1.
Loch (locha, lochannan) 1. loch.
Lochan (lochain, lochain) 1. pond.
Long (luinge, longan) 2. ship.
Luidhear (luidheir, luidhearan) 1. chimney.

M

Ma, if.
Ma ta, truly, indeed, well then.
Mac (mic, mic) 1. son.
Maduinn (maidne, maidnean) 2. morning.
Magadh (magaidh) 1. derision, mockery.
Maighstir (maighstir, maighstirean) 1. master.
Mairi, 2. Mary.
Maise, 2. beauty.
Maiseach, beautiful.
Mal (mail, malan) 1. rent.
Maol, bald, hornless, blunt.
Maor (maoir, maoir) 1. steward, factor.
Maor-taighe, house factor.
Mar, as, like.
Mar sin, thus.
Mar tha, already.
Mar thachair, how or what happened.
Masladh (maslaidh, maslaidhean) 1. reproach, disgrace.
Math, good.
Mathair (mathar, mathraichean) 2. mother.
Meall (mealladh) deceive.
Mealladh (meallaidh) 1. deceit.
Meall (mill, meallan) 1. lump, cluster.
Mearachd, 2. error.
Meas, 1. esteem.
Meas (measa, measan) 1. fruit.
Meirle, 2. theft.
Meirleach (meirlich, meirlich) 1. thief.
Miann (miann, miannan) 2. desire.
Milis, sweet.
Mill (milleadh) spoil, destroy.
Mo, my.
Monadh (monaidh, monaidhean) 1. hill-pasture, moorland.
Mor, big, great.
Morag, Morag.
Moran, much, many.
Mort (muirt, muirt) 1. murder, massacre.
Mothaich (mothachadh) feel, notice.
Mu, about.
Mu ochd uairean, about 8 o'clock.
Muinntir (muinntreach) 2. people.
Muir (mara, marannan) 1. sea.
Mur (often followed by An, am) unless, if not.

N

Na, the, when more than one is meant.
Na reverses an order word. Na buail! do not strike!
Nach, that not.
Nach, introduces a question.
'Na theine, on fire.
Na h-uile, everyone, all. A h-uile fear, every man.
Neach sam bith, anyone at all.
Nam, if ; also Nan.
Ni, shall or will do.
Ni (ni, nithean) 1. thing.
Nigh (nigheadh) wash.
Nighean (nighinne, nigheannan) 2. girl, daughter.
Nollaig (Nollaige, Nollaigean) 2., Christmas.

O

O or **Bho,** from, since, because.
Obair (oibre or oibreach, oibreachan) 2. work, labour.
Obair-uisge, 2. waterworks.
Ochd, eight.
O chionn, ago, because ; also A chionn.
O chionn fada, a long time back.
Oillteil, dreadful.
Oir, for.
Ol (ol), drink.

Olc, bad, evil.
O'n taigh, from home.
Ord (uird, ordan) 1. hammer.

P

Pailt, plentiful.
Pailteas (pailteis) 1. plenty, abundance.
Paipear-naigheachd (paipeir, paipearan, followed by naigheachd) 1. newspaper.
Pairc (pairce, paircean) 2. park.
Paisde (paisde, paisdean) 1. and 2. child.
Partan (partain, partanan) 1. small crab.
Pathadh (pathaidh) 1. thirst.
Peadair, Peter.
Peann (peanna or pinn, peanntan) 1. pen.
Peigi, Peggy.
Peiteag (peiteig, peiteagan) 2. waistcoat, short sleeved jacket.
Piob (pioba, pioban) 2. pipe, bagpipe.
Piobair (piobair, piobairean) 1. piper.
Piuthar (peathar, peathraichean) 2. sister.
Poit (poite, poitean) 2. pot.
Pos (posadh) marry.
Posadh (posaidh, posaidhean) 1. marriage.
Posta (posta, postachan) 1. postman.
Priosanach (priosanaich, priosanaich) 1. prisoner.
Punnd (puinnd, puinnd) 1. pound in weight or sterling.

R

Radh, saying ; also a saying. 1.
Rainig, reached.
Rathad (rathaid, rathaidean) 1. road.
Reic (reic), ,sell.
Ri, ris, at, to, etc.
Righ (righ, righrean) 1. king.
Righ Deorsa, King George.
Rioghachd (rioghachd, rioghachdan) 2. also Righeachd, kingdom.
Ri mire, playing.
Rinn, made, did.
Riomhach, elegant, handsome.
Ro, rather much, extremely.
Roimh, before.
Roimh fhada, before long.
Rop (ropa, ropan) 1. rope.
Ruadh, reddish.
Ruairidh, Roderick.
Rud (ruid, rudan) 1. thing, matter.
Ruig (ruigsinn) reach.
Ruith (ruith) run.
Runair (runair, runairean) 1. secretary ; also Runaire.
Ruraich (rurach), search.

S

Saighdear (saighdeir, saighdearan) 1. soldier.
Salach, dirty.
Samhach, quiet.
Saor (saoir, saoir) 1. joiner, carpenter.
Saor, free.
Saorsainneachd, 2. joinery, carpentry.
Sasunn (Sasuinn) 1. England.
Sasunnach (Sasunnaich, Sasunnaich) 1. Englishman: also English.
Seachad, past.
Seadh, That's so.
Seall (sealladh), look.
Sealladh (seallaidh, seallaidhean) 1. sight, view.
Sean or **seann,** old.
Seanmhair (seanmhar, seanmhairean) 2. grandmother.
Searrag (searraige, searragan) 2. bottle.
Seas (seasamh), stand.
Seinn (seinn), sing, play on instrument.
Seo, this.
Seol (seoladh) sail.
Seol (siuil, siuil) 1. sail.
Seoladair (seoladair, seoladairean) 1. sailor.

Seomar (seomair, seomraichean) 1. room.
Seumas, James.
Sgailean-uisge, 1. umbrella.
Sgairteil, lively, energetic.
Sgaoil (sgaoileadh), spread, disperse, dismiss.
Sgeir (sgeire, sgeirean) 2. low rock in sea, skerry.
Sgian (sgeine, sgianan) 2. knife.
Sgeul (sgeoil, sgeoil) 1. story.
Sgeulachd (sgeulachd, sgeulachdan) 2. story, tale.
Sgian agus sgor, knife and fork.
Sgith, tired.
Sgoil (sgoile, sgoilean) 2. school.
Sgoilear (sgoileir, sgoilearan) 1. scholar.
Sgoilt (sgoilteadh) split.
Sgriobh (sgriobhadh), write.
Siabunn (siabuinn) 1. soap.
Sid, yon, that.
Sil (sileadh), rain, drip.
Sin, that.
Sin (sineadh) stretch.
Sine, Jean.
Siol (sil) 1. seed.
Sios, downwards.
Siucar (siucair) 1. sugar.
Slainte, 2. health.
Slan, whole, healthy.
Slat (slaite, slatan) 2. rod ; yard in length.
Sluagh (sluaigh, sluaighean) 1. crowd, people, public.
Smaoinich (smaoineachadh), think.
Sneachd (sneachda) 1. snow.
Socair (socrach) 1. ease.
Socaireach, easy.
Sochair (sochaire, sochairean) 2. boon, benefit.
Soitheach (soithich, soithichean) 1. vessel of any kind.
Solus (soluis, solusan) 1. light.
Spainnteach (Spainntich, Spainntich) Spaniard, Spanish.
Spairn (spairne) 2. effort, struggle.
Spion (spionadh), pluck, snatch.
Spog (spoige, spogan) 2. claw, hand of timepiece.
Sporan (sporain, sporanan) 1. purse. Sparan is rare.
Srac (sracadh), tear. Sracte, torn.
Sraid (sraide, sraidean) 2. street.
Sron (sroine, srointean) 2. nose, headland.
Sruighlea, Stirling.
Sruth (srutha, sruthan) 1. stream.
Stol (stoil, stolan) 1. stool.
Stad (stad), stop.
Stob (stuib, stoban) 1. stake.
Stocainn (stocainn, stocainnean) 2. stocking.
Suas, upwards.
Sud, yon.
Suidh (suidhe), sit.
Suidheachadh (suidheachaidh) 1. situation.
Suil (sula, suilean) 2. eye, glance.
Suim (suime) 2. respect, heed.
Sunnd, 1. joy.

T

Tagair (tagradh), claim, plead.
Taic (taice, taicean) 2. support.
Taigh (taighe, taighean) 1. house.
Taigh-dhealbh, 1. picture-house.
Taigh-osda, 1. inn.
Taillear (tailleir, taillearan) 1. tailor.
Tarrang (tairngne, tairngnean) 2. nail.
Tairneanach (tairneanaich) 1. thunder-clap.
Talamh (talmhainn, talamhan) 1. earth.
Talla (talla, tallachan) 1. hall.
Taobh (taoibh, taobhan) 1. side.
Tapadh leat, leibh, thank-you.
Tarruling (tarruing), draw, pull.
Tart (tairt) 1. thirst.
Te, 2. person or thing.
Teachdair (teachdair, teachdairean) 1. missionary, messenger.
Teann, tight.
Tearlach (Tearlaich) 1. Charles.
Teas, 1. heat.
Teine (teine, teintean) 1. fire. 'Na theine, on fire.

Teth, hot.
Tha, am, is, etc.
Thachair met: from Tachair meet.
Thainig, came.
Thall, beyond, on the other side.
Theagamh, perhaps.
Thig, shall come; also Come!
Thoir, give, bring.
Thug, gave, brought.
Thuirt, said.
Tig, will come (after gun nach, etc.).
Tighinn, coming.
Till (tilleadh) come.
Tilg (tilgeadh) throw.
Tinn, sick.
Tinneas (tinneis, tinneasan) 1. sickness, disease.
Tioram, dry.
Tir (tire, tirean) 1. land.
Tog (togail) lift.
Toil (toile, toilean) 2. will, desire.
Toileachas (toileachais) 1. pleasure, satisfaction.
Toilichte, pleased.
Toinisg (toinisge) 2. sense.
Toirt, giving, bringing.
Toit (toite) 2. smoke.
Tomadach, bulky.
Tombaca, 1. tobacco.
Tormod or **Tormoid,** Norman.
Traigh (traghad, traighean) 2. shore, beach.
Trath, early.
Trath (traith, traithean) 1. meal; also time.
Treabh (treabhadh), plough.
Treas, third.
Treis, 2. a while.
Tri, three.
Troimh, through.
Trom, heavy.
Trus (trusadh) gather.
Tuathanach (tuathanaich, tuathanaich), 1. farmer.
Tubaist (tubaiste, tubaistean) 2. accident.
Tugha, 2. thatch.
Tuig (tuigsinn), understand.
Tuilleadh also tuillidh, more.
Tuit (tuiteam) fall.
Tur (tuir) 1. understanding, sense.
Tusa, thou, emphatic.

U

Uasal, noble, well-born.
Uasal (uasail, uaislean) 1. gentleman, nobleman.
Ubh (uibhe, uibhean) 2. egg; also spelt Ugh.
Ubhal (ubhail, ubhlan) 1. apple.
Ud, yon, that.
Uile, all, every.
Uilleam (Uilleim), William.
Uinneag (uinneige, uinneagan) 2. window.
Uisdean, Hugh, but Eoghann in Argyll.
Uisge (uisge, uisgeachan) 1. water, rain.
Ullaich (ullachadh) prepare.
Umhal, obedient.
Upraid (upraide, upraidean) 2. racket, confusion: also ubraid.

www.ingramcontent.com/pod-product-compliance
Lightning Source LLC
La Vergne TN
LVHW010545100826
845148LV00013B/2611

* 9 7 8 1 5 7 9 7 0 5 4 9 7 *